WINE:

From Neolithic Times
to
the 21st Century

WINE:

From Neolithic Times

to

the 21st Century

Stefan K. Estreicher

Algora Publishing
New York

No portion of this book (beyond what is permitted by
Sections 107 or 108 of the United States Copyright Act of 1976)
may be reproduced by any process, stored in a retrieval system,
or transmitted in any form, or by any means, without the
express written permission of the publisher.
ISBN-13: 978-0-87586-476-1 (trade paper)
ISBN-13: 978-0-87586-477-8 (hard cover)
ISBN-13: 978-0-87586-478-5 (ebook)

Library of Congress Cataloging-in-Publication Data —

Estreicher, Stefan K., 1952-
  Wine: from Neolithic times to the 21st century / Stefan K. Estreicher.
    p. cm.
  Includes bibliographical references and index.
  ISBN-13: 978-0-87586-476-1 (trade paper: alk. paper)
  ISBN-13: 978-0-87586-477-8 (hard cover: alk. paper)
  ISBN-13: 978-0-87586-478-5 (ebook)
  1. Wine and wine making—History. I. Title.

  TP549.E88 2006
  641.2'209—dc22

                              2006022780

Printed in the United States

This book is dedicated to those who are continuously curious about life, and occasionally thirsty.

Like Miguel de Cervantes, Stefan K. Estreicher "drinks wine when there is an occasion, and sometimes when there is no occasion."

Unlike Miguel de Cervantes, he is a professor of Physics at Texas Tech University.

TABLE OF CONTENTS

FOREWORD

Wine is one of the foundations of Western civilization. The story of wine is that of religion, medicine, science, war, discovery, and dream. It is foolish to believe that this story can be told in a few pages, or even in several thousands. After all, entire books have been written on short periods of history, specific wine regions, or even single vineyards. Yet I was tempted to try and, once again, found the strength to yield to temptation.

My goal is to give an overview of the history of wine through the ages: from its humble beginnings in Neolithic times through Antiquity and the Middle Ages; then its expansion from Europe to the rest of the world, the major scientific and technical discoveries, the man- and nature-made catastrophes around the turn of the 19th century, and the slow emergence of modern wines after World War II. Of course, many things happened in the past 7,000 years, and this book must remain short, informative, and easy to read. One big challenge is to pick what to include and what to leave out. Forgive me for skipping a few centuries here and there. Another challenge is to select the level of detail. There are longer and more complete books on the subject, in particular Hugh Johnson's *Vintage*[1] and Rod Phillips' *A Short History of Wine*[2]. Relatively recent archeological finds have shed considerable light on the origin and early history of wine. Patrick McGovern's *Ancient Wine*[3] is fascinating for those curious about early wines and winemaking. He also co-edited a book[4] discussing numerous technical issues. I have incorporated information from these and many other sources in my book.

---

1. H. Johnson, *Vintage* (Simon and Schuster, New York, 1989).
2. R. Phillips, *A Short History of Wine* (Harper Collins, New York, 2000).
3. P.E. McGovern, *Ancient Wine* (Princeton University Press, Princeton 2003).
4. *The Origins and Ancient History of Wine*, ed. P.E. McGovern, S.J. Fleming, S.H. Katz, (Gordon & Breach, Amsterdam, 2000).

I also benefited from more direct help. Jim Brink, professor of history at Texas Tech, had the pleasure of correcting the historical aspects of the book. Edward George, professor in the Classical Languages Department, searched the writings of Latin authors such as Julius Caesar, looking for "wine" and "wooden barrels." Kristin Reid downloaded satellite data and drew the maps. Thanks are also due to many generous friends. Michel Baly, in Alsace, opened his impressive wine cellar, shared some of his wines with me, and then guided me to some spectacular vineyards and wineries in the region. Luca Bellinelli never missed an opportunity to take me to small wineries in northern Italy. Amanda Chavira patiently proofread the manuscript. Many other friends encouraged and helped me over the years, and I owe thanks to all. There will always be wine for you in my cellar.

May this book entice you to search further and discover more of life through this unique window: the story of wine.

> *One not only drinks wine, one smells it, observes it,*
> *tastes it, sips it, and one talks about it.*
> *—Edward VII (1841-1910)*

CHAPTER 1. IN THE BEGINNING...

*"Bacchus": a convenient deity invented by the Ancients as an
excuse for getting drunk.*
— *Ambrose Bierce (1842-1914?)*

Wine, beer, and mead are ancient alcoholic beverages. Wine is special because neither barley nor honey spontaneously ferments. On the other hand, it is impossible to cultivate grapes and not end up making some kind of wine. The reason is that yeast lives on the skin of grapes. Squeezing mature grapes into a jar releases grape juice. Given an appropriately warm temperature, the yeast feeds on the sugar and breaks it into alcohol and carbon dioxide. The population of the desirable yeast, *saccaromyces cerevisiae*,[1] quickly develops in the sweet and water-rich grape must, and completely dominates any other yeast populations once the alcohol content exceeds 5% or so. After a couple of days, there is wine: not a Château Lafite, but wine nonetheless. Making great wine is an art, making good wine is a science, but the fermentation of grapes is a natural and unavoidable process. Yeast is abundant in the foam that develops on the surface of fermenting wine grapes. This foam can be used to initiate the fermentation of other fruits such as dates, or honey (if water is added), or barley. The latter produces beer. For this reason, it is most likely that wine pre-dates beer and other alcoholic beverages, although probably not by much.

---

1. There are 15 genera of yeast, one of which is *Saccharomyces* (literally sugar-fungus). *S. cerevisiae* is one of 7 species, and tolerates about 14% alcohol. *S. bayanus* has a higher alcohol tolerance, *S. rouxii* a higher sugar tolerance, etc. There are many strains of *S. cerevisiae*, such as *Torulaspora delbrueckii*, which will be mentioned later in this book. *S. cerevisiae* is also the yeast used in bread and beer. A different strain of *S. cerevisiae* grows under the bark of oak trees and the soil around them (Science **309**, 375 (2005).

The fermentation of grapes is accidentally discovered, then planned, early in the Neolithic period, roughly 8000 BCE, as mankind first establishes permanent settlements. People domesticate animals and cultivate the land. In the Near East, the earliest-known clay pots that can be used for preserving seeds from one planting season to the next, and protecting them from rodents and birds, appear about 6000 BCE.

THE IMPORTANCE OF WINE TO THE ANCIENTS

Beyond giving man the first alcoholic buzz and hangover, wine quickly becomes a very important part of life, as well as death. Indeed, 4,000-year-old burial chambers contain vine cuttings (still intact) in silver sleeves, probably in the hope that vineyards can be planted in the afterlife. Such artifacts are at the Georgian State Museum in Tbilisi. But wine affects the living in many ways. It is of course a social lubricant and provides an occasion to celebrate. Socrates enjoys the *symposium*, literally "drinking together." He delights in discussing philosophy with his followers while drinking wine, and develops the reputation of being able to outlast his guests. The Greek symposium is for men only.

More importantly, wine is safe to drink and has many medical benefits, especially as an antiseptic. This is particularly important in times when nothing is known about infection and disease. The mysterious properties of wine are magical and lead to a wide range of religious beliefs. It is always tempting to invoke supernatural powers to explain natural phenomena one fails to understand. Finally, many business opportunities are associated with all the aspects of the wine trade.

Wine is safe to drink

The establishment of permanent settlements raises the issue of safe drinking water. This is not just a problem of ancient times. Today, whenever wars or natural disasters displace people into temporary camps, getting clean water is an immediate concern. The reason is that water is easily contaminated when groups of people settle for an extended period at a given place. The risk of dysentery, cholera, and other water-born diseases is high, unless water is filtered, boiled, or chemically treated. In Neolithic times, wine could be used. Indeed, if the grape juice contains enough sugar, the natural fermentation can produce a wine with as much as 15% alcohol by volume. That is three or four times more than beer, and enough to kill many harmful bacteria. Late harvesting, and adding honey or sweet fruits to the must, increase the sugar content. Mixing wine with water (typical water-to-wine ratios range from 2-1 to 5-2) can be a lifesaver. This is so important that it becomes the normal way to drink wine for thousands of years.[2] While it is not true that the Ancients *always* mix wine with water, there is plenty of evidence to suggest that this is a very common practice indeed. The Bible provides one counter-example (Isaiah 1.21-22):

> *How the faithful city has become a harlot!...*
> *Your silver has become dross, your wine mixed with water.*

However, such an uncompromising condemnation of mixing wine and water is the exception. Greek law is first codified[3] by Zaleucus of Locris, about 650 BCE, 30 years before Draco of Athens and "Draconian law." Zaleucus claims to have received the laws from Athena, the goddess of war. He states: *if anyone drinks unmixed wine without a physician's prescription to effect a cure, the penalty is death.* Under Draco's laws, stealing grapes is also punishable by death.

In De Re Militari, the 4th century Roman military writer Flavius Vegetius warns that armies must not use "bad or marshy water, for the drinking of bad water is like poison." Later, he writes "If a large group stays too long ... in one camp, the water becomes corrupt." Similar advice persists throughout history. Disease devastates numerous armies after wine (and vinegar) runs out and the troops drink contaminated water. Historians such as Lemmert emphasize the correlation between a poor vintage and the outbreak of disease. One example deals with the year 1602: "There was a severe winter, a cold April, a hailstorm in the summer. The wine was scarce and of poor quality. In this year, there was plague in the Palatinate, through Saxony and Prussia." Beverages made with boiled water, such as coffee or tea, become popular in the West only in the 1600s. Vallee quotes Frederick the Great who, in 1777, is upset at his soldiers for drinking coffee: "His Majesty was brought up on beer, and so were his ancestors and officers. Many battles have been fought and won by soldiers nourished on beer, and the King does not think that coffee-drinking soldiers can be relied upon to endure hardships in case of war."

There are many references to wine and water in the Bible, such as a famous wedding during which water is changed into wine, a feat earlier attributed to Bacchus. Noah takes vine cuttings with him on the Ark and plants a vineyard as soon as possible after the Flood. He obviously knows how to do it and why, a

---

2. B.L. Vallee in *Alcohol in the Western World* (Scientific American, June 1998) has discussed the role of wine and beer as everyday drinks from the earliest days of Western Civilization to the 17th century.
3. This is mentioned in 228 CE by Athenaeus of Naucratis in *Deipnosophistai*, 10.429.1, ed. C. B. Gulick (Loeb Classical Library, Cambridge, 1928). This book contains many wine quotations.

point ignored by Benjamin Franklin who credits Noah with being the first to plant vines:

> 'Twas honest old Noah first planted the Vine,
> And mended his Morals by drinking its Wine;
> He justly the drinking of Water decried;
> For he knew that all Mankind, by drinking it, died.

Although the Muslims refrain from consuming alcohol, the Qur'an[4] recognizes the importance of wine, in particular when describing the gardens of paradise (Surah 47.15). Note that "water," "pollution," and "wine" occur in the same sentence:

> A similitude of the Garden which those who keep their duty [to Allah] are promised:
> Therein are rivers of water unpolluted, rivers of milk whereof the flavor changeth not,
> rivers of wine delicious to the drinker, and rivers of clear-run honey.

Mixing wine and water still occurs today in Catholic churches, during mass. The symbolism of this gesture goes back to the very roots of western civilization.

Wine and medicine

Wine is the most powerful antiseptic available until the Arabs invent distillation in the late 9th century. Then alcohol from distilled wine (then fruit or grain) takes its place in medicine, until penicillin is manufactured in quantity during World War II. Records of medical uses of wine date back over 4,000 years. Wine stimulates digestion and prevents disease. The cloth covering wounds is soaked in wine to help prevent infection. The "Ebers Papyrus," dated -1500 BCE, reveals that the Ancient Egyptians sometimes rely on beer mixtures as remedies.

Hippocrates, the father of medicine, believes that disease is not a punishment from the gods but has natural causes. Therefore, natural means can cure it. Hippocrates recommends different types of wines to treat different ailments. He even advises[5] that "infants should be... given their wine diluted and not at all cold" and specifies which wine should be given to infants.

---

4. *The Glorious Qur'an*, translated by M.M. Pickthall (Tahrike Tarsile Qur'an, Elmhurst, 1999).
5. Hippocrates of Kos, *Regiment for Health*

Figure 2: Hippocrates of Kos (460-375 BCE).

Much later, Plutarch (45-125 CE), a priest of the Delphic Oracle, writes that wine is the most useful of all drinks, the sweetest-tasting medicine, the most pleasant of foods. In the Middle Ages, it is believed that drinking wine in which the bones of a saint have been dipped cures lunacy.[6] French scientist Louis Pasteur (1822-1895) calls wine "the most healthful and most hygienic of beverages." Wine is certainly more healthful than most of the water available until the 20th century.

Modern medicine recognizes the health benefits of (moderate) wine drinking, even though there are few quantitative and systematic studies. In Europe, a daily glass of red wine is often recommended to treat mild anemia; a class of chemicals, *flavonoids*, antioxidants in grape skins, appears to have many beneficial properties; other chemicals, *polyphenols*, prevents[7] heart disease, arteriosclerosis, and maybe some cancers; anticancer agents are also found[8] in wine aged in oak casks. But there is also documented evidence[9] of the negative impact of excessive or long-term drinking.

The gods of wine

Since the earliest times, gods have been associated with nature, fertility, harvest, vines, wine, even the wine press. The *Oxford Dictionary of Ancient Deities*[10]

6. A.D. White, *A History of the Warfare of Science with Theology in Christendom* (Prometheus, Buffalo, 1993), Chapter XIII, Sec. VIII.
7. Angewandte Chemie (international edition), research news alert (48) **42**, 6012-6014 (2003).
8. Chemical and Engineering News, October 31, 2005, p. 36
9. A. Estreicher, Prolune, October 2005 (SwissProt, Geneva, at *http://www.expasy.org/prolune*)
10. P. Turner and C.R. Coulter, *Dictionary of Ancient Deities* (Oxford U. Press, 2000). See also I. Aghion, C. Barbillon, and F. Lissarrague, *Gods and Heroes of Classical Antiquity* (Flammarion, Paris, 1994).

lists 36 such gods. They play important roles in most ancient civilizations around the Mediterranean basin. The best-known god of wine is Bacchus,[11] an ancient deity who becomes Dionysus in Greece then Bacchus again in Rome, where he is later associated with excessive drinking and revelry. Many other gods have the same or similar attributes: Bassareus to the Lydians, Tarhunta to the Hittites, Aramazd and Hayk (or Hayik) to the Armenians, Dusares in Arabia and the list goes on: Antheus, Bromius, Iacchus, Iakhos, Lenaidos, Zagreus. In Egypt, Osiris is the goddess of wine and protectress of brewers.

The earliest Greek wine festivities, the *Anthesteria*, evolve into *Dionysia* in Athens, then *Bacchanalia* in Imperial Rome, where they degenerate into (very) wild events. Today, there are still numerous wine festivities throughout Europe at vintage time, and some likeness of the ancient Bacchus often participates.

Figure 3: Gallo-Roman bronze of young Bacchus found in Vertillum (today Vertault, Cote d'Or, France). (Photo courtesy of J.L. Coudrot).

In Roman (and Greek) mythology, Jupiter, the god of thunder and lightening, has an affair with Semele, a woman from Thebes. This greatly upsets Jupiter's wife, Juno. She convinces Semele to demand that Jupiter appears in front of her in all his glory — that is, as thunder and lightening. This occurs indoors, and the pregnant Semele does not survive the event. Jupiter saves the unborn Bacchus by sewing him into his own thigh, and later delivers the baby himself. Thus, Bacchus is a half-god, born out of the thigh of Jupiter, something very special indeed, and a virgin birth.

The associations of grapes with life and of wine with religion do not stop when Emperor Constantine replaces the worship of the sun by Christianity. Jesus and the saints appear with halos around their heads, as if they are standing in front of the sun. The vine is associated with the cross in many places, such as the oldest European university, in Bologna, founded in 1086. The "Mystic Wine Press,"

11. A. Dalby, *Bacchus: A Biography* (Getty, Los Angeles, 2003).

8

a stained glass window in the Church of Sainte Geneviève in Paris, shows Christ on the cross pressing on the wine press. His blood mixed with wine flows for the faithful. Wine, the blood of the vine, is a central part of the Eucharist. Cardinal Ratzinger, now Pope Benedict XVI, refers to himself as "a humble worker in God's vineyard." The shadow of Bacchus still floats over the Eternal City.

Figure 4: A vine-cross combination at the University of Bologna. (Photo SKE)

Wine and trade

Wines and winemaking offer many business opportunities. One can buy and sell wine of course, but also vine cuttings, clay jars, resin for coating the inside of the jars, as well as a wide range of herbs and spices used to perfume a wine or mask its low quality. There is also transportation. Wine and the associated technologies give rise to a trade that flourishes since the earliest days. The archeological evidence for it is abundant.[12] Clusters of grapes and/or wine gods are prominent on many ancient coins.[13]

---

12. P.E. McGovern, *Ancient Wine* (Princeton University Press, Princeton 2003).
13. The book by P.R. Franke and I. Marathaki, *Wine and Coins in Ancient Greece* (The Hatzimichalis Estate, Athens, 1999) contains many reproductions of coins, wine-related citations by ancient authors, and details about the types of wines produced in various regions of ancient Greece.

Trade is most likely how wine spreads from isolated Neolithic villages to the entire Near East, then all around the Mediterranean basin. Numerous ancient texts mention wines, vineyards, and the wine trade. An early example is the Code of Hammurabi (1795-1750 BCE). He reigns in Babylon and produces the earliest publicly displayed laws. His code consists of 282 articles, three of which discuss taverns, held by women, and the wine trade:

> [108] If she overcharges for wine, she will be drowned; [109] if conspirators meet in a wine shop and are not delivered to the court, the tavern-keeper shall be put to death; [110] if a "sister-of-god" opens a wine-shop or enters a wine-shop to drink, she shall be burnt to death.

Figure 5: Athena and a bunch of grapes (Cilicia-Soloi) 390-370 BCE (courtesy Zach Beasley)

ARCHEOLOGICAL EVIDENCE OF WINE

The evidence of wine and winemaking since the early Neolithic to the classical Greek period has been detailed by Patrick McGovern.[14] Much of the data comes from the analysis of organic residue in ancient jars, using Fourier-transform infrared (FTIR) absorption spectroscopy, gas or liquid chromatography, DNA analysis, and other tools. A few micrograms of material suffice to detect trace amounts of chemicals. In an FTIR experiment, the material under study, exposed to light, absorbs only those frequencies that are in resonance with selected normal-mode frequencies of the chemicals in the sample. The spectra consist of sharp vibrational lines characteristic of specific chemical bonds, such as the stretch and wag modes of a particular C-H bond in a particular organic compound. Neutron activation analysis involves neutron irradiation. Some nuclei absorb the neutrons, become radioactive, and their decay provides the unique atomic composition, and hence a "fingerprint," of the clay. This allows its geographical origin to be pinpointed. With these and other microscopic tools, archeology has become quantitative in many respects.

---

14. P.E. McGovern, *Ancient Wine* (Princeton University Press, Princeton 2003).

Figures 6-7: Hammurabi's code in the Louvre museum in Paris, with enlarged detail. (© Art Resource, New York).

The archeological proof of wine-making, even wine technology, has been unearthed in several Neolithic sites in the Zagros Mountains of North-Eastern Iran. The oldest site to date, *Hajji Firuz Tepe*, uncovered during the archeological expedition of Mary M. Voigt from the University of Pennsylvania Museum, is dated 5400-5000 BCE.[15] In Farsi, "*tepe*" (or rather, "*tappe*") refers to a small hill or mound, something an archeologist would dig up when looking for ancient sites.

Archeologists found six wine jars, each about 10 inches tall with a capacity of about 2.5 gallons, with clay stoppers nearby. The residue in the jars includes tartaric acid and its salt, calcium tartrate. Tartaric acid is the principal acid of grapes and crystals of tartaric acid form in wine. Although a few other plants, such as the baobab tree, also produce tartaric acid, no such plants grow in that region. In the Near East and at that period, tartaric acid can only come from grapes. Wine drinkers often see tiny crystals of tartaric acid on the sides or bottom a glass, especially if the wine is a few years old. The crystals look like tiny grains of salt. The German name for them is *Weinstein*, literally "wine-stone."

---

15. P.E. McGovern, M.M. Voigt, D.L. Glusker, L.J. Exsner, Nature **381**, 480 (1986). See also footnotes 3 and 4.

Figure 8: One of six wine jars from Hajji Firuz Tepe. (© University of Pennsylvania Museum)

The presence of crystals of tartaric acid proves that wine was kept in the jars for some months, if not a year or longer. Ancient jars found at numerous archeological sites in modern Turkey, Georgia, Iran, Egypt, Gaza, and other locations show similar traces of tartaric acid.

Who made the very first wine and precisely where will probably never be established. However, it is now certain that some 7,000-8,000 years ago, wine drinkers populated the region between the Black and Caspian Seas down to the northern Zagros Mountains. Pottery shards of age comparable to the Hajji Firuz Tepe jars, found nearby in what is now the Republic of Georgia[16] also show traces of tartaric acid. Winemaking has survived there ever since.

The very first Neolithic wine, pre-dating Hajji Firuz Tepe, was probably made from the native *Vitis vinifera sylvestris* vine. "Vitis" means that it is a vine, "vinifera" that, when mature, its fruit contains enough sugar to make wine (at least 10%), and "sylvestris" that it grows near trees as the vine needs support. This vine still grows wild around the Mediterranean basin and continental Europe. Pollen cores from Lake Urmia, just north of Hajji Firuz Tepe, prove that *v.v. sylvestris* did grow in the region at the time.

---

16. R. Ramishvili, Hist. Archeol. Ethnol. Art Hist. Ser. 2, 125 (1983) and P.E. McGovern (unpublished).

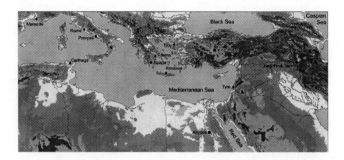

Figure 9: Some of the ancient cities and sites mentioned in the text (map: Seiichi Nagihara, graphics: Ed Youngblood).

Figure 10: Following Joseph Stalin's death in 1956, over 450 bottles of Georgian, French, and Spanish wines are taken away from Moscow. Forty years later, they are found in a cellar in Tbilisi, Georgia, a region where wine was first produced over 7,000 years ago (photo Reuters).

V.v. sylvestris is dioecious (sexual). Most plants are either male or female, with just a few percent self-pollinating hermaphrodites. However, cultivation leads to the elimination of the male plants, which produce no fruit, then of the female plants, which are no longer pollinated. Soon, the cultivated vines consist mostly of hermaphrodites. Their pips have a distinct shape and are larger than the female pips of *v.v. sylvestris*.[17] Large concentrations of hermaphrodite pips are an archeological proof of grape cultivation. These cultivated hermaphrodite vines evolved into *vitis vinifera vinifera*, to which nearly all of today's wine-producing cultivars belong.

Figure 11: The wild v.v. sylvestris still grows today, this one in Germany along the Rhine River. (photo: Andrew Walker, UC Davis)

Another residue in the Hajji Firuz Tepe jars, and other ancient wine jars, is resin from the terebinth tree. The inside of the jars is coated with it. This coating waterproofs the jar but, more importantly, this particular resin has antibacterial properties. Its presence slows down the growth of *acetobacter aceti*, the bacteria that turn alcohol into acetic acid, the main component of vinegar. Pliny the Elder calls the resin of the terebinth tree the "best and most elegant resin." Its presence in a wine jar preserves the wine much longer than would be possible without it. Later, the Romans use myrrh and resins from exotic trees such as frankincense to preserve (and perfume) their wines.

Resinating the wine by partially or fully coating clay jars is done systematically throughout Antiquity, and this resin is widely traded. Today's remnant of the tradition of resinating wine is the Greek *Retsina* wine. In this case, resin of a pine tree (*Pinus Halepensis*) is added to the must in order to give it a special flavor. The Greeks themselves rarely drink this. It is for tourists.

Thus, the history of wine begins at the end of the last major Ice Age, with the first Neolithic settlements near the Black and Caspian Seas, a region which encompasses today's southern Georgia, eastern Turkey, Armenia, Azerbaijan, and northwestern Iran.

FIRST LARGE-SCALE EXPANSIONS

Viticulture quickly expands from isolated Neolithic villages to the entire Middle East and North Africa, probably through trade. By the time of the Phoenicians, vineyards and the wine trade flourish on the eastern shore of the Mediterranean Sea.[18]

---

17. A. Leonard Jr. in *The Origins and Ancient History of Wine*, ed. P.E. McGovern, S.J. Fleming, and S.H. Katz (Gordon and Breach, Amsterdam, 2000).

18. P.E. McGovern, *Ancient Wine* (Princeton University Press, Princeton 2003).

In the 5th century BCE, the Greek historian Herodotus of Halicarnassus (484-432 BCE) describes the wine trade from Armenia down the Euphrates and Tigris rivers. He uses *bikos phoinikeiou* to describe the vessels used in this transport. Some authors[19] translate this as "casks of palm wood." However, McGovern points out that Herodotus is probably talking about Phoenician amphorae. The Celts deserve the credit for the invention of wooden casks and barrels.

The most important traders of the ancient world are the Phoenicians. These sailors and merchants first appear around 3200 BCE. By 2500, they populate the eastern coast of the Mediterranean Sea, from today's Syria through Lebanon, down to northern Israel. They trade timber (most famously, Lebanese cedar), metals, wines, vines, and other commodities, all around and beyond the Mediterranean basin. Ultimately, they even reach the Atlantic coast of North Africa as well as the British Isles, where they purchase tin from Cornwall, a metal needed to alloy with copper to make bronze. Around 1200 BCE, they invent the first alphabet consisting of single letters. The Greek alphabet derives from it.

They do not call themselves "Phoenicians." Instead, they associate with city-states such as Byblos, Sidon, Tyre, or Beirut. However, the Greeks call them *Phoinikes* — the purple people — for they produce a rare and very expensive purple fabric. They extract tiny amounts of dye from a gland of the murex mollusk: a single pound of the precious dye requires some 60,000 mollusks. Wearing clothes of this color symbolizes great wealth and power. Today, Cardinals still dress in purple.

In 1110 BCE, the Phoenicians lay the foundations of the port city of Cadiz, very near Jerez, where sherry is made today. Even though vines are probably cultivated in the Iberian Peninsula before their arrival, the Phoenicians contribute in terms of technology and trade. Their presence in Portugal, on the Atlantic coast of Europe, is documented as early as 1000 BCE. They establish commercial outposts in Cyprus, Sicily, Corsica, and other key locations. In 814, the Phoenicians from Tyre establish the city of Carthage (from *Qart-hadasht*, new city), a few miles north of today's Tunis. They bring wines, vines, and their understanding of viticulture everywhere they go.

The Phoenician dominance ends in 332 BCE, as Alexander the Great crushes their allies, the Persians, and then destroys the city of Tyre. The Phoenicians of Carthage fight against Rome over control of Sicily: the Punic wars begin in 264 and end in 146 BCE with the destruction of Carthage.

The Phoenicians deserve a good part of the credit for the first large scale and systematic expansion of viticulture. The Greeks are next. They establish colonies and bring with them not just vines but also their knowledge of viticulture.

---

19. Herodotus, *The Histories*, translated by G.C. Macaulay and revised by DE. Lateiner (Barnes and Noble Classics, New York, 2004), I.194.

They refine the art of making sweet and longer-lasting wines. Finally, the Romans invade much of Europe and plant many vineyards inland. They need wines to supply their troops. The next major expansion of viticulture, worldwide this time, begins more than 1,000 years after the fall of Rome, as vine cuttings and seeds accompany the Spanish Conquistadores to Central and South America, then make their way to Texas and California. Later, the Dutch introduce vines in South Africa and the British in Australia.

CHAPTER 2. WINE IN EGYPT, GREECE AND ROME

Quickly, bring me a beaker of wine, so that I may wet my mind
and say something clever.
                    —Aristophanes (448-385 BCE)

EGYPT

The history of Dynastic Egypt covers over 3,000 years. If one includes the pre-dynastic period (4500-3100 BCE), the time span exceeds 4,500 years. Wines have been a part of that history at least since the end of the pre-dynastic period. Indeed, some 700 wine jars have been found in the tomb of Scorpion I, dated 3150 BCE and located in Abydos, a few hundred miles south of the Nile delta. The residue in the jars includes tartaric acid and resin from the terebinth tree. A number of jars also contained grape skins and pips, as well as sliced figs. They could have been added to the must during the fermentation to increase the sugar content (and therefore the amount of alcohol after fermentation) or to the finished wine simply to flavor it. There is also DNA evidence[1] of the presence of the yeast *Saccharomyces cerevisiae* in some jars. Neutron activation analysis shows that the jars do not come from Egypt but southern Palestine and the Jordan valley. It is possible that the wine was also imported. There is no evidence for *v. vinifera* in Egypt until about 2700 BCE.

---

1. D. Cavalieri, P.E. McGovern, D.L. Hartl, R. Mortimer, and M. Polsinelli, J. Mol. Evol. **57**, S226 (2003)

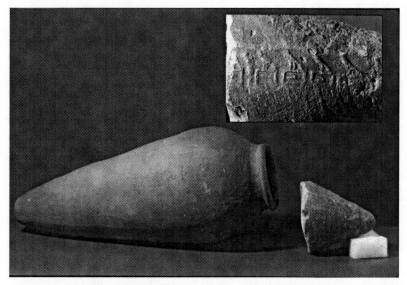

Figure 12: One of the ~700 amphorae from the tomb of Scorpion I, in Abydos. The marking on the clay stopper is enlarged (©University of Pennsylvania Museum).

The presence of wine in the tomb suggests that it was a very important part of life, important enough to follow the ruler into the afterlife. It also suggests that it was a luxury item, reserved for the upper class. The considerable volume (700 jars) indicates that wine had already been a part of Egyptian life for some time.

In contrast to the earliest wine jars, which are broad, the Abydos jars are elongated and have the pointed tip characteristic of amphorae. The markings on some of the clay stoppers describe the type of wine, its production date, region, as well as the name of the winemaker: the same information one finds on today's wine labels. Egyptian, Phoenician, Greek, and Roman amphorae are very often marked to indicate their content, geographical origin, and sometimes the name of a producer or a company "logo." The marking on the stopper of one amphora in the tomb in King Tut reads: *Year 5. Wine of the House-of-Tutankhamen Ruler-of-the-Southern-On, l.p.h (in) the Western River, by the chief vintner Khaa.* The fact that the vintage year is indicated suggests that the better Egyptian wines are aged in amphorae for years.

The production of wine in Ancient Egypt is concentrated mainly near the Red Sea and in the Nile Delta. However, wine is also imported, as noted by Herodotus:[2] "into Egypt from all parts of Hellas [Greece] and also from Phenicia are brought twice every year earthenware jars full of wine..." Whether produced locally or imported, wine is a costly luxury in Ancient Egypt, accessible only to the upper class. Vineyards are owned by the elite. They require extensive manpower, irrigation, and costly winemaking facilities. The common people drink beer. Bread and beer are an important part of the diet of most people. Wine is drunk during festivities, used in magic or religious rituals, medicine, and as offerings to gods. In addition to Osiris, the Egyptians worship Shezmu, deity of the wine press; Renenutet, deity of vineyards and winemaking; and Hathor, goddess associated with drunkenness: "a perfect year begins with drunkenness."[3]

Figures 13-14: Markings on Greek amphora handles (-300 BCE) indicating the origin of the wine: at left Rhodes, with the head of Helios, the sun-god, a represen-

tation of the famous Colossus, at right Themisonium (from the author's collection).

We do not know how the Egyptian wines tasted or which types of grapes were used, but recent and widely-circulated new releases indicate that Tutankhamen enjoyed red wine. Ms. Guasch-Jane and Professor Lamuela-Raventos, from the University of Barcelona, tested part of a wine jar from King Tut's tomb[4] for the presence of malvidin-3-glucoside, the chemical that imparts color to red wine. Direct testing is not feasible but the scientists exposed the sample to a basic solution that causes malvidin to break down into syringic acid, which is detectable. They point out that there had been clues to the wine preferences of the ancient Egyptians, such as dark-colored grapes depicted on murals in old tombs. In fact, there is no evidence that white wine, as we know it, was available except for sweet wines, which become amber in color with age.

The key contributions of the Egyptians to wine are technological. In particular, the Egyptians are credited with the invention of the amphora. A typical amphora has thick walls, as much as one inch, and a pointed tip, which allows it to be partially buried in sand. For storage, amphorae are normally laid on their side to keep the (clay) stopper from drying and shrinking. The inside of the amphora is partially or fully coated with resin. Note that the Greeks and the

2. Herodotus, *The Histories*, translated by G.C. Macaulay. revised by DE. Lateiner (Barnes and Noble, New York, 2004), III.6.
3. Part of a song inscribed on a wall of the temple of Hathor at Philae. See L. Oakes and L. Gahlin, *Ancient Egypt* (Barnes and Noble, New York, 2003).
4. The tomb, dated 1300 BCE, contained 26 wine amphorae.

Romans usually coat only the neck[5] and use additives other than the resin of the terebinth tree to slow down the oxidation of the wine.

With only minor changes in shape and the additions of handles, amphorae are used by everybody: the Egyptians, Phoenicians, Greeks, Romans and others. Wooden barrels appear quite late, in the first century CE. Thus, for over 5,500 years, the material of choice to ferment, transport, store, and age wine is clay (jars and amphorae).

Figure 15: Part of the Nina de Garis Davies (1881-1965) painting of a mural in the tomb of Khamwaset, pure-priest of Amenhotep I, second king of the 18th Dynasty, c. 1520 BCE. The harvest, foot-treading, and pouring of wine into amphorae for fermentation are shown. Several amphorae are represented with holes in their necks. The holes allow the carbon dioxide gas to escape during the fermentation. (Theban tomb 261, ©The Trustees of The British Museum.)

The Egyptian winemaking technique is painted on the walls of several private tombs. The workers pick the grapes, which are then treaded by foot. The must is poured into amphorae which, when full, are stoppered with clay. The mouth of the jar would be filled with reeds or other materials to allow carbon dioxide to escape during the fermentation. Then, it would be permanently sealed with a (marked) lump of clay. Alternatively, small holes in the neck of the amphora allow the gases to escape and then are sealed with clay. The wine is ready to age, sometimes for many years.

---

5. P.E. McGovern, private communication.

The Egyptians also discover glass, sometime in the second millennium BCE.[6] Glass-making technology is closely related to metallurgy. Both involve furnaces, high temperatures and the manipulation of molten materials. Glass is silica (sand) and metal: The higher the metal content, the lower the melting temperature. The Egyptians' main source of metal for glass is sodium carbonate (*natron*).[7] They discover that adding trace amounts of specific metals to the melt produces glass of various colors: a little gold for red, cobalt for blue, etc. The Egyptians import cobalt from Persia specifically for that purpose. They produce colored glass beads and small but elaborate glass jars for perfume and other precious liquids. They manufacture the glass jars by covering a clay shape with frit (bits of solid glass), heating it to melt the glass, and then removing the clay after the glass solidified. However, they do not produce sturdy bottles of the type needed to keep wine.

The Phoenicians expand the Egyptian technology and mass-produce glass cups for wine drinking. They invent glass blowing around 100 BCE. Later, the Romans make (rather opaque) windowpanes, as well as vases and sophisticated decanters. However, their glass is neither clear nor transparent — the kind of glass we are familiar with today — because of impurities in the raw material and poor temperature control. None of the glass produced by the Romans is sufficiently thick and strong to make anything resembling wine bottles, either. The first really transparent (and fragile) glass, *cristallo*, is manufactured in the 15th century on the island of Murano, off Venice, Italy. This achievement involves purified source materials, elevated temperatures maintained long enough for impurities to diffuse out, and temperature control during cooling. The first sturdy bottles date back to 1630s and the first large-scale (industrial) production of wine bottles to the early 1900s.

GREECE

The oldest traces of Greek civilization are found on a group of islands in the south Aegean Sea — the Cycladic civilization, and the island of Crete — the Minoan civilization. By about 2000 BCE, the Minoans live in cities, dominated by Knossos on the northern coast of Crete. They speak a language different from Greek and their writing has yet to be deciphered. They farm, trade, practice bull jumping, and... drink wine. In contrast to Egypt, where wine is drunk by the wealthy, wine in Greece is accessible to everybody. The earliest Greek clay

6. See J.L. Mass, M.T. Wypyski, and R.E. Stone, Materials Research Society Bulletin **26** (2001), p.381; G. Sarton, *Ancient science through the Golden Age of Greece* (Dover, 1993); L. Sprague de Camp, *The Ancient Engineers* (Barnes and Noble, New York, 1993).
7. Deposits of sodium carbonate (CO_3Na_2) exist at Wadi Natrum in Low Egypt and at Elkelab in High Egypt.

tablets mention olive oil and wine, a combination at the heart of Greek (then Roman) cultures. The cultivation of olives and grapes requires 160 to 180 days of work per year, allowing for leisure time, something still appreciated today by Mediterranean people, justifiably so.[8]

The grapes are often treaded by foot in large baskets or small stone treading vats, and the juice is collected in clay jars for fermentation. There is archeological evidence that the Minoans ferment a mixture of wine, barley beer and honey, together. Barley contributes starch and honey adds sugar to the natural sugar in the grapes. The combination certainly results in a sweet wine with high alcohol content. Indeed, the winemaker has no way of stopping an ongoing fermentation, which continues until the alcohol content becomes too high for yeast to survive, probably around 15%.

A surprising twist to this story is that residue of the same wine-beer-honey blend is found in the tomb in King Midas, about 60 miles from Ankara (Turkey), dated 700 BCE, that is at least 800 years later and 500 miles away. A reproduction of this drink is "Midas touch," produced by the Dogfish Head Brewery.

Figure 16: This brew of Muscat wine, barley beer and honey, is a possible replica of a drink appreciated in Minoan Crete and at King Midas' funeral (courtesy: Dogfish Head Brewery).

---

8. The archeology of ancient presses for wine and olive oil wine is discussed in detail in Brun J.-P., *Le vin et l'huile dans la Méditerranée antique* (Errance, Paris, 2003) ; Brun J.-P., *Archéologie de l'huile et du vin* (Errance, Paris, 2004).

In 1500 BCE, an earthquake followed[9] by the catastrophic eruption of the volcano on the Greek island of Strongphyle, destroys these civilizations, or at least dramatically weakens them. An invasion by the Myceneans follows and the Minoan civilization disappears. The Myceneans establish colonies throughout modern Greece. These colonies are independent of each other and often engage in armed confrontations. Around 1250 BCE, the Myceneans unite and go to war against the city of Troy. Homer writes his epic tales of this war some three centuries later.

During the 12th century, the Mycenaean dominance gradually diminishes. This civilization succumbs to a Dorian invasion from the north. The much less civilized Dorians extinguish the light of the Mycenaean civilization and usher in the "Greek Dark Ages," which last some 450 years.

The "classical" Greek civilization emerges in the 8th century BCE with city-states such as Argos, Corinth, Thebes, Sparta, and Athens. This marks the beginning of Greece as a major power in the ancient world. Like in Mycenean times, there is no overall king, ruler, or central power in Greece. The city-states, ruled sometimes by a counsel and sometimes by a tyrant, are proud of their independence and often fight each other. This independence leads to their greatness and then to their demise. The environment creates a fertile ground for a large number of scientists, poets, historians, and other thinkers to thrive. They appear not just in Athens (Socrates, Plato, Aristophanes,...) but also elsewhere in Greece and its colonies: Democritus of Abdera, Herodotus of Halicarnassus, Hippocrates of Kos, Archimedes of Syracuse, just to name a few. Pythagoras, born on the island of Samos, still famous today for its Muscat wine, moved to Croton in Southern Italy.

The Athenians invent democracy. It is limited by today's standards, since only free male residents participate. They enjoy public debate and seek the pleasures of life, including wines. Sparta is very different. Drinking and the cult of Dionysus are not a priority. The men spend most of their lives in the army, and are dedicated to Sparta, over their own lives. The Spartans are feared because defeat, surrender, or even retreat is unthinkable. A Spartan is victorious, or dead. The heavy infantry fights in a tight formation called the phalanx (it will be borrowed by the Romans). Each man, armed with a long spear and protected by a shield, is willing to die defending his position.

A variety of wines is produced throughout Ancient Greece. Each region, each island, has its own style and reputation. For example, the wines from Chios, Lesbos, Naxos, and Thasos have excellent reputations. The dark wine from the island of Kos is often sold mixed with salt or seawater *(leukokan wine)*. One is hard pressed to find a poet, philosopher, or writer who never mentions wine or vineyards.[10] Aristotle calls the wines from Rhodes *powerful though less delicate than those*

9. The precise date of the volcanic eruption is debated.

from Lesbos. The first century writer Diodorus Siculus, best known for his description of Atlantis, writes that the wines from Thracian Maronea are so thick and heavy that they are drunk diluted with up to 20 parts of water! Socrates practices the symposium, during which he and his male[11] companions debate and drink. Democritus, the philosopher famous for formulating the atomic theory of matter and believed to have lived to the age of 100, claims to know all the Greek varieties of grapes. That this should be understood as a claim to fame suggests that they are many.

Wine is widespread and commonly drunk at all levels of society. A typical breakfast in Athens consists of bread soaked in wine. The Greeks drink wine for pleasure, but also because they believe that it improves digestion and preserves health. According to Greek mythology, wine is a gift from the gods — a gift that Dionysus (Bacchus) generously spreads to common mortals during his travels and tribulations.

In order to produce wines with a high percent of alcohol (they age longer) a variety of techniques are developed to increase the sugar content in the grapes. This includes late harvest, of course. One can also leave the clusters of grapes to raisin in the sun, twist the stems on the vine to stop the flow of sap, or boil the must to evaporate the water and concentrate the grape juice, which is then added to wine to strengthen it. Some winemakers add honey, or fruits such as dates or figs to the wine. Sweet and powerful wines are normally drunk mixed with water. This mixing is done in a *krater* — a wine-mixing vase. Wine is added to the water in the krater, and the mixture is served to the guests. This way, everybody drinks the same mix. Plutarch recommends two measures of water for one measure of wine, a "composition which removes what is harmful without taking out what is useful."

However, sweet wines are expensive. The poor drink lesser wines, often obtained by squeezing through a piece of cloth what is left in the treading vat after the first-run juice is extracted. Such wines have a short lifespan. A few light dry white wines are also produced. Hippocrates recommends those for specific medical conditions. Wines are sometimes aged for years and honey, lime, and/or a variety of spices added to them: oregano, cinnamon, cumin, saffron. Other additions seem strange: rose petals, perfumes, or even gypsum! One can speculate that some of these additions help mask odd flavors or disguise the smell of an oxidized wine on its way to becoming vinegar.

Wine laws are first enacted on the island of Thasos in the mid-5th century BCE. They regulate the minimum quality of wine. Later laws (-425-400 BCE)

---

10. Extensive quotes about wine are in the books by Johnson, Phillips, and Franke-Marathaki.
11. The Greeks, and later the Romans, consider drinking the affair of men. Women are discouraged from it.

deal with the earliest allowed harvest date, in order to insure that only mature grapes are used.

The Greeks export viticulture to every settlement they colonize. They arrive in Sicily very early, in the 8th century BCE. Sicilian wines such as *Mamertine*, maintain a reputation of excellence for centuries.[12] From Sicily, the Greeks establish colonies in southern Italy, where Etruscan wines already exist. In 600 BCE, the Phocaeans[13] land their warships at the mouth of the River Rhône in southern Gaul and establish the city of Massalia, today Marseille. They teach the Gauls how to prune vines, thus enhancing the yield. The Greeks also venture north along the cost of the Black Sea and establish vineyards in (what are now) Bulgaria, Romania, Moldova, and even Ukraine. These territories will become the Roman Tracia (south of the Danube River) and Dacia.

While the Greek influence is strongest along the coast of the Mediterranean basin, there is a piece of evidence that they also trade deep inland. During the winter of 1952-53, a huge bronze krater is unearthed at Mont Lassois, between Paris and Beaune, in the tomb of a Celtic princess (or priestess[14]) who died around 500 BCE. The krater of Vix, richly decorated in typical Greek style, is 5'4" tall and has a capacity of 260 gallons. Excluding its massive handles, the krater is made of a thin sheet of bronze (1.2mm thick) and weighs only 120 lbs or so. It is the largest such krater ever found, including in Greece. The restoration of the krater in 1954 provided no evidence of any kind of residue. Although there is no evidence of any wine production in the region at the time (the first Burgundy vineyards date back to Roman times, some five centuries later) there is abundant evidence that the region is a center of international trade. It is a major producer of iron, and the very important tin from Cornwall is shipped from southwest England up the River Seine to that region. The krater, manufactured in a Spartan colony of southern Italy, could have been exchanged for tin, as the Greeks needed to make bronze for weapons and shields during the wars against the invading Persians.

The Greeks reach the peak of their civilization with Plato (428-347 BCE) and Aristotle (384-322 BCE). Athens becomes the leading military and trading power of the ancient world after defeating the superpower of the day, the Persians. The Athenians first defeat King Darius on land at Marathon (490 BCE). Darius' son Xerxes seeks revenge and invades Greece with an army of some 200,000 Persians. With great difficulty, he defeats the Spartan Leonidas at Thermopylae, where 300 Spartans fight to the death against Xerxes' huge army. The Persians burn the (abandoned) city of Athens, then are routed by the Athenian

---

12. Sicily still produces very interesting wines today, including dessert wines such as Zibibbo, a Muscat.
13. Phocaea was a Greek city in western Anatolia, Turkey.
14. J. Davies, *The Celts* (Cassell, London, 2002).

Themistocles at the naval battle of Salamis in 480 BCE. The Athenians rebuild their city and prosper for fifty years.

Figures 17-18: The krater of Vix (courtesy J.L. Coudrot, Musée du Châtillonais, Châtillon sur Seine, France), with enlarged detail showing the typically Greek style decoration (courtesy: museeduchâtillonnais@wanadoo.fr, Châtillon sur Seine, Côte d'Or 21, France).

In 431 BCE, for no good reason as far as we know, Athens initiates a war against Sparta. It ends with Athens' surrender in 404. This war devastates Athens and severely weakens Sparta, just when a new force emerges in northern Greece. Philip of Macedonia takes hold of the entire country. His son, Alexander the Great, known to be a heavy wine drinker, destroys the Persian Empire and conquers huge territories, including northern India and key parts of Egypt. His empire crumbles following his death in 323 BCE. In the meantime, Rome is expanding. It will overcome Greece in 146 BCE and Egypt in 31 BCE. For centuries, the Romans praise Greek wines, and the trade in Greek wines continues long past the Roman invasion.

ROME

Rome, the Imperial power that would dominate Western Europe (including England), the Near East, and North Africa by the end of the 1st century CE, has humble beginnings. The legend says that the twin brothers Romulus and Remus, raised by a she-wolf, lay the foundations of the city in 735 BCE. Rome is first ruled by Romulus, then by six consecutive Etruscan kings, with the advice of a senate. In 510 BCE, the senate deposes the last king, the despised Tarquin the Proud, and invents the Republic. Two consuls, elected for one year, replace the king.[15] They share the executive branch of government. In case of crisis, the senate appoints a dictator with extended powers, for the duration of the crisis.

At first, Rome expands its territory by conquering — or rather, assimilating — central and southern Italy, where the Romans encounter the Greek colonies. They are exposed to high-quality Greek wines, the technology associated with them, and the Greek god of wine, Dionysus. He quickly becomes Bacchus to the Romans and joins the Roman mythology. The cult of Bacchus, with its drinking, singing, dancing, and revelry does not fit well with the traditional Roman values of discipline, stoicism, honor, and dedication to Rome. Tolerated for while, the cult is made illegal by the senate in 186 BCE. It continues nonetheless. The ban survives until the end of the Republic, when Julius Caesar, realizing that the cult of Bacchus cannot be eliminated, makes it official.[16] It thrives until Christianity becomes the official religion of the Empire during the reign of Theodosius I.

The most critical conflict during the days of the Republic involves Sicily, a Carthaginian colony. The first two Punic Wars (264-241 and 221-202) test the Roman navy (Archimedes' "claw" sinks Roman ships besieging Syracuse) then its army (Hannibal crosses the Alps with elephants and attacks Rome from the north). Despite Rome's victory, Cato the Elder (234-149) insists: *Cartago delenda est!* (Carthage must de destroyed). The Roman army destroys the city in 146 BCE. By that time Rome controls Italy, North Africa, Greece, and the Iberian Peninsula. Plutarch[17] describes Cato as a stoic, who drinks water unless he is extremely thirsty, in which case he mixes it with vinegar. When strength fails him, he drinks wine...

During the Kingdom and much of the Republic, the Greek influence in winemaking and drinking dominates. The preferred wines are sweet with high alcohol content. They are drunk mixed with water. The local production is not — or not perceived to be — as good as the Greek imports. The Romans add resin, herbs, spices, and perfumes to many wines. Often, the purpose is to mask the bad taste of a vinegary wine.[18] The amphorae must be kept airtight, which is achieved with a cork or with a clay stopper. The amphorae themselves are sometimes fumigated with rosemary and other plants.

At the turn of the first century BCE, several Roman vineyards gain popularity and respect. The most famous of them is *Falernum*. Its wine, praised by many authors, is sometimes aged for 20 years or more. The Falernum is one of

---

15. The Romans date years by the names of the two consuls elected that year. In his *Ecclesiastic History of the English Nation*, the venerable Bede (673-735) from Jarrow proposes to set year 0 as Anno Domini (AD).

16. S.J. Fleming, *Vinum* (Art Flair, Glenn Mills, 2001). This book contains detailed information about the production of wine, amphorae and wine presses, drinking habits, shipping data, and other facts.

17. A.H. Clough and J. Dryden: Plutarch, *The Lives of the Noble Grecians and Romans* (Modern Library, New York, 1932).

18. S.J. Fleming, *Vinum* (Art Flair, Glenn Mills, 2001).

*Figure 19: The Roman amphora also has a
pointed tip (photo SKE).*

Julius Caesar's favorite wines. The others ones are the Greek wines from Lesbos and Chios. The reputation of the Falernum survives for centuries. Gregory of Tours mentions it some 150 years after the fall of Rome.

However, the bulk of the wine produced is not of Falernian quality. The best wines are obtained by collecting the drops oozing from a pile of grapes under their own weight.[19] A lower quality, but still very good wine is obtained by treading the grapes by foot, a process that extracts a lot of tannins and color in a short 10-12 hours. This is done today for some of the best Ports in Portugal. After treading, the crushed grapes go into the winepress,[20] a technology greatly expanded by the Romans. The simplest press involves boards and levers; the most sophisticated one is the screw press.

---

19. This is the so-called *vin de goutte*. In French, "goutte" means "drop." This process is still used today to produce the Tokaji Esszencia.
20. S.J. Fleming, *Vinum* (Art Flair, Glenn Mills, 2001).

Figure 20: Some famous vineyards near the end of the Roman Republic. The city of Pompeii is just south of the Vesuvius and Rome is slightly inland from the Setinum vineyards (map: Kristin Reid).

The most important Roman shipping ports are Ostia — the port of Rome, and Pompeii. The volume of goods is substantial. A site in Rome called Monte Testaccio is a 150-feet tall mountain of broken amphorae, which provides valuable information about shipping during the late years of the Republic. Wine is imported from the Provinces, mostly Spain and North Africa, and traded with Celtic populations in Northern provinces and southern France. The Romans notice that transporting wine by sea sometimes improves it.[21]

---

21. English merchants re-discover this in the 1600s when shipping port wines from Portugal to England via the fishing waters off Newfoundland. Portuguese explorers also find that the crude wine produced on the Madeira Islands improves substantially by shipping through the tropics and the equator.

Figure 21: Roman mosaic from Saint Romain-en-Gal, France, 3rd century.
(Musée des Antiquités Nationales, St.-Germain-en-Laye;
photo Erich Lessing, © Art Resource, NY)

Many Roman authors discuss in detail wines, viticulture, cultivars, pruning, aging, and winemaking. Of particular notice are Cato the Elder,[22] Columella,[23] and Pliny the Elder.[24] By the time of Columella, the amphorae are no longer systematically resinated. The Greek techniques to achieve powerful, sweet wines are expanded by the Romans. This includes late harvesting, stem twisting, and allowing the clusters of grape to over mature or even raisin on beds of straw before making the wine. Today, a similar technique is still used in France to make the *vin de paille*, while in Italy, clusters of Trebbiano and Malvasia grapes are hung in basements for several months. The grapes lose some 60% of their water. The resulting *Vinsanto* wines are incomparable. Another sweet and most delicate Roman wine called *passum* is obtained by soaking raisins in wine.

22. Marcus Porcius Cato (234-149 BCE) writes the first book on agriculture, *De Agri Cultura.*
23. Iunius Moderatus Columella (4-70 CE) expands on viticulture in *De Re Rustica.*
24. Caius Plinius Secundus (23-79 CE) writes the extensive *Naturalis Historia.* The entire 14th volume is dedicated to wine and viticulture. Pliny claims that some 50 top-quality varieties of grapes grow in Italy.

Today's descendent of this wine is the *Passito*, made with almost dry Muscat grapes on the small island of Pantelleria, between Sicily and North Africa. But all the sweet and powerful wines, whether imported from Greece or produced in Italy, are expensive and in short supply.

Figure 22: A rendering of amphorae ready for shipping (photo SKE).

Cato, Pliny, and Columella also describe another way to sweeten a wine: boil the must down to one-quarter or even one-half of its original volume, then add the resulting syrup to wine in concentrations of the order of 1:30. Cato recommends boiling in copper or lead vessels. Pliny[25] favors lead over copper, as the latter imparts an unpleasant taste to the wine. Columella recommends that only

25. Strangely, Pliny also states that the boiling down must be done during a moonless night (XIV.136).

lead vessels be used, coated with oil. Howeder, drinking the resulting wine causes lead poisoning.[26] This affects almost exclusively the wealthy, as only they can afford such expensive wines.[27]

Figures 23-24: At Rome's Ostia Antica, the harbor of Ancient Rome, dolia are found standing (top, surrounding Professor Mario Capizzi) as well as buried. The old harbor is now six miles away from the sea (photo: Capizzi).

26. For details and references see http://penelope.uchicago.edu/-grout/encyclopaedia_romana/wine/leadpoisoning.html .
27. The use of lead to sweeten and preserve wine (lead inhibits the growth of bacteria) continues in Europe well into the 18th century, in spite of increasing evidence of its toxicity. Widespread use of sugar begins when sugar cane cultivation, with slave labor in European colonies such as Brazil, provides inexpensive sugar to the European market.

Among Roman technological advances is the *dolium*, a huge clay jar with a capacity of about 300 gallons. It is used for shipping or is buried up to its neck in the ground for fermentation and storage. Burying the huge vessel reduces the risk of cracking during the fermentation, and then helps minimize the temperature fluctuations during storage. Wine taverns, common in cities such as Rome and Pompeii, store their wine in dolia. The Romans also improve glass-making techniques and manufacture sophisticated, albeit fragile, wine decanters.

Rome and the size of the territory it controls keep increasing. In 300 BCE, the population of the city of Rome is about 100,000. It is close to one million by the turn of the first millennium. Fleming[28] estimates that in the 1st century CE, the demand for wine is 23 million gallons per year, and that each citizen and soldier consumes some 100 gallons of wine per year. Wine truly is for everyday drinking, by everybody. Even slaves are given rations of wine, albeit the lowest quality and diluted.

Civil unrest and struggle for power mark the last decades of the Roman Republic. The elected consuls have much more power than granted by the old constitution, and they control the army. Going to war is an opportunity to maintain power and control. In 59 BCE, Julius Caesar is named Consul. A year later, he invades Gaul, defeats the Celts[29] and, four years later, lands in England. Upon his return, Caesar refuses to dismantle his army before reaching Rome, as is expected, and crosses the river Rubicon. Another civil war begins. Caesar defeats his archrival Pompey. In 46 BCE, he becomes the undisputed ruler of Rome. Two years later, he is assassinated and civil war starts again. Caesar's nineteen-year-old great-nephew, Octavian, triumphs over Anthony and his ally Cleopatra. With the title Augustus, he becomes the first de-facto Emperor of Rome. He develops a professional bureaucracy and imposes peace over the Empire. It lasts until his death in 14 CE. Over 50 emperors rule Rome until 476, when the Goth Odoacer sacks Rome and forces the sixteen-year old Romulus Augustulus to abdicate.

With Julius Caesar, the Romans move for the first time in large numbers into regions that are not accessible by ship. Goods such as wine must be transported overland. The army needs wine, a lot of wine. The common soldiers normally drink a low quality, sour wine called *posca*, or even vinegar. But water is not safe to drink. With few or no roads, transporting heavy and breakable amphorae is most impractical.

---

28. S.J. Fleming, *Vinum* (Art Flair, Glenn Mills, 2001).
29. The Celtic people live in most of Europe since long before Roman times. The various groups have much in common but no central ruler. Independent populations are no match for the Roman armies. Vercingetorix unites the Celts against Caesar but is defeated. Some Celts assimilate; others retreat to Brittany and western England.

The Celts use wooden barrels. Caesar himself hardly notices this: the Latin word for wooden barrel, *cupa*, is mentioned[30] only once in his writings and then not in conjunction with wine. However, someone notices, and wooden barrels begin to replace amphorae, at first for overland transport. By the fall of Rome, amphorae are no longer in use in Western Europe, except in the south — Sicily and many Greek islands — as well as the Near East. The use of wooden barrels for wine marks an important turning point in this story. Wines had been fermented, aged, transported, and stored in clay jars for over 5,500 years. Now, wood replaces clay. Wine does not age in wood nearly as long as in clay.

The Romans plant vineyards throughout Europe in the first and second centuries. Except for the coast of the Mediterranean Sea, where viticulture exists since long before Roman times, many of today's European vineyards are planted by the Romans. The major reason for planting vineyards is to supply the Roman garrisons. In many regions, viticulture already exists and the Romans simply expand the vineyards and bring their technology. This is the case in Hispania (today Spain and Portugal), southern Gaul (southern France), Tracia (mostly Bulgaria and the European part of Turkey), and Dacia (modern Romania and part of Ukraine and Moldova). In other regions, there is no evidence of viticulture predating the arrival of the Romans, as in central and northern France, along the river Rhine, or in southern England. At first, the vines are always planted on the southern slopes of hills: Hermitage, Sancerre, Montagne de Reims, etc. The idea is that southern exposure favors the production of traditional-style wines. Since vines and olives are always cultivated together, it is not yet known that vines can prosper in climates too cold for olive trees.[31]

There is something new about the vineyards planted in Gaul. They are not located along a warm coastal region, bathed in sunshine much of the year. Instead, they are inland, as far north as England, where growing seasons are short and winters harsh. The grapes produce less sugar; the wines cannot be made heavy and sweet as those from Greece or Italy. These new wines are light, dry, and more acidic. At first, they are considered to be inferior, but people's tastes evolve. By 200 or so, light wines are very popular as far south as Rome itself.

Around 40 or 50 CE, the Romans establish the port-city and its surrounding vineyards of *Burdigala* (Bordeaux). The primary purpose of a shipping port on the Atlantic coast is to supply the Roman legions in England with wine and other goods. The wines from the region have a good reputation early on. Ausonius, the 4th-century Roman poet, is one of many who writes about this

---

30. E.V. George, Department of Classical Languages and Literatures at Texas Tech University, private communication.
31. Brun J.-P., *Le vin et l'huile dans la Méditerranée antique* (Errance, Paris, 2003); Brun J.-P., *Archéologie de l'huile et du vin* (Errance, Paris, 2004).

region and praises its wines. He even owns a vineyard in (or near) today's town of St. Emilion. One of the best Bordeaux wines is named after him in 1781.

Figure 25: The fabulous Château Ausone named after the Roman poet Ausonius (courtesy: Château Ausone).

On August 24, 79 CE, a massive eruption of Mount Vesuvius destroys the cities of Pompeii and Herculaneum, the nearby vineyards, and all the wine warehoused in Pompeii. Pliny the Elder dies in the event. Pliny the Younger tells that the survivors see daylight for the first time only three days after the eruption. The cities are not rebuilt nor the vineyards replanted.[32]

The eruption of the Vesuvius severely disrupts the wine trade for years. A great demand for wine ensues and new vineyards, cash crops, are planted everywhere, often at the expense of food crops. The result is a collapse of the price of wine and a shortage of grain, which threatens Rome's food supply. The situation became so serious that in 92, Emperor Domitian bans the planting of new vineyards in Italy and orders half the vineyards in the provinces be converted for food crops. Widely ignored, this edict is repealed in 280 by Emperor Probus, in an attempt to restore economic stability in Gaul.

The Roman Empire begins to crumble in the late 4th century. There are too many provinces to administer, too many miles of frontier to defend, too many hordes of aggressive barbarians pushing against the eastern and northern borders of the Roman Empire. It begins around 375 with the Huns. Other warriors from the Far East displace the Goths, originally a peaceful tribe. They seek refuge on Roman territory south of the Danube River, and convert to Chris-

---

32. In 1996, a joint project involving the Italian wine producer Mastroberardino and the Archeological Superintendent of Pompeii identify the location of some of the Roman vineyards and the cultivars used. In 1999, they produce a few cases of "Pompeii wine": 85% Piedirosso, 15% Sciascinoso.

tianity. However, the Romans abuse and mistreat them. Under the command of their king, Alaric, they rebel, overpower the Roman army, sack Rome for three days in 410, and then migrate to the Iberian Peninsula, where they are called Visigoths ("Goths of the West").

Figures 26-27: Emperors Domitian (81-96, left) and Probus (276-282, right) (courtesy: Zach Beasley, beast-coins@vcoins.com).

The Roman Empire splits into an Eastern Empire centered in Constantinople and a Western Empire centered in Milan, then Ravenna. With the Edict of Milan in 313, Emperor Constantine (285-337) restores to the Christians any confiscated property and grants them the tolerance that other religions enjoy. After 320, soldiers have to attend church parades and the Sun God no longer appears on Constantine's coins. Constantine declares himself a Christian in 324. Emperor Theodosius I (346-395) makes the faith the official state religion.

The European climate, warmer than today in the 3rd and 4th centuries, is changing. Vineyards, successful as far north as Belgium and southern England, are gradually abandoned. A long period of misery is just around the corner. The floodgates of the barbarian invasions open on a very cold night of December 406. The Rhine freezes solid. The barbarians cross it by foot at Mainz, sack the city, and move on. Seventy years later the Western Roman Empire falls. The wines from Bordeaux, no longer needed, are forgotten for almost seven centuries. The Eastern Empire survives another thousand years. Ironically, one of the aims of the barbarians who sack Rome is to "be like the Romans": Rome has been the symbol of power, wealth, and civilization for centuries. Now it is gone.

CHAPTER 3. DARK AGES, LIGHT WINES

Quand le vin est tiré, il faut le boire.
— *Ancient French saying*

EARLY MIDDLE AGES IN WESTERN EUROPE

As the Roman Empire crumble, waves of Slavs, Alamans, Franks, Vandals, Goths, Huns, and others invade various parts of Europe and fight for land and power. Attila the Hun devastates much of Europe for a decade, until his death in 453. Europe is a mess: battles, lootings, massacres, no laws or order, little or no political or economic stability. However, many of the invaders become Christians, are exposed to wine, and encourage viticulture. Some of them make alliances with the Romans, on occasion. In 451, Theodoric I, king of the Visogoths, establishes a kingdom that includes Aquitaine (Bordeaux) in the north and a good part of Spain. In 451, he joins the Romans and they defeat[1] Attila the Hun in Châlon (Champagne). The enlightened Ostrogoth[2] Theodoric the Great (454?- 526) takes Ravenna in 493. He becomes the *de facto* ruler of much of what was the Western Roman empire. His reign is characterized by relative political and economic stability, artistic and architectural achievements, and remarkable religious tolerance — a sign of civilization absent in much of today's world. The Ostrogoths are expelled from Italy shortly after his death.

Everyday life abruptly changes in much of Europe. In the days of the Roman Empire, there was a professional bureaucracy, laws, roads, and sufficient security to trade goods between distant parts of the Empire. For example, pieces of amphorae marked with the seal of the Spanish vintner Lucius Quintus Sec-

---

1. Theodoric falls off his horse and is trampled to death by his cavalry.
2. The "Ostrogoths" are the "Goths of the East."

37

ondus are found as far north as Hadrian's Wall,[3] which runs across northern England. When Rome collapses, nobody is left to enforce laws, maintain roads, or guarantee safety for commerce.

The weak have no choice but seek the protection of the more powerful, in exchange for some fee or, more commonly, goods and services. The more powerful seek protection from even more powerful lords, again in exchange for money, goods, or military service. This extends all the way to the king, who cannot be king without military power, revenues, and an administration. The result is the feudal system in which everyone's role is essentially set a birth. At the bottom of society are the serfs, bound to the land, then peasants who can move to another region, albeit with permission. Serfs and peasants who grow wheat or vines must rent the mill or winepress, which belong to the local lord. Next are small landowners, artisans and merchants. At the top are various levels of nobility, who often practice warfare with their neighbors, and the clergy, who is in charge of souls. The bishops are appointed by the king.

Church law applies to moral matters, and local custom for purely secular and local legal issues. Over the centuries, some local markets and fairs gain a reputation, attract people from a wider area, and become large markets. These towns grow into cities, and centers for business and manufacturing. This evolution involves trade on a larger scale. Merchants need laws appropriate for business. Irnerius (1055-c.1130), founder of the school of law at the University of Bologna, modifies Justinian's Roman law to serve that purpose. Banks appear. However, this takes place some 600 years after the collapse of the Western Roman Empire. It takes a long time for a middle class to emerge.

That anything of the old system survives at all after the fall of Rome is remarkable. However, Latin remains the language of choice for official functions, not just in the Church but also in government and, later, in Universities.[4] The Christian Church not only survives the fall of Rome but actually gains strength. It is rather well organized, with a hierarchy, an administration, monasteries, and land. In 496, king Clovis converts to Roman Christianity, and all the Franks follow. Thus, early on, the Church enjoys the protection of kings and emperors. Its power will rarely be challenged until the French Revolution of 1789.

Kings and others in the higher nobility also enjoy the wines produced by monks. In 587, King Guntramn, grandson of Clovis, gives a vineyard to the abbey of St. Benignus near Dijon. In 630, the Duke of Lower Burgundy gives several vineyards to the abbey of Bèze, in the heart of Burgundy. These will become the famous Gevrey, Vosne, and Beaune.

---

3. S.J. Fleming, *Vinum* (Art Flair, Glenn Mills, 2001).
4. Isaac Newton writes the *Principia* in Latin in 1686, but then *Optiks* in English, a language more accessible to the public. The professors at Collegium Majus, the old University in Krakow (Poland), lecture in Latin as late as the 18th century. The Catholic Church still uses Latin today for encyclicals.

Vineyards are established in much of Europe and the Near East. A few belong to the secular nobility but most belong to churches, abbeys, and monasteries.[5] Although wine is needed for mass, only a small fraction of the production is used for that purpose. The clergy has land, patience, abundant and cheap manpower. The founder of western monasticism,[6] St. Benedict (480-547), establishes precise rules governing the life of monastic men and women. The Order of Saint Benedict is named in his memory. Chapter 31 of his Rules reads, under the title "What Kind of Man the Cellarer of the Monastery Should Be,"

> [a]s cellarer of the monastery, let there be chosen from the community one who is wise, of mature character, sober, not a great eater, not haughty, not excitable, not offensive, not slow, not wasteful, but a God-fearing man who may be like a father to the whole community.

In his *History of the Franks*[7], Gregory (539-594), 19th bishop of Tour, gives an account of everyday life and major events during the early Middle Ages. He describes violent death by murder or torture often and in detail, as if it were a natural cause of death. He also casually mentions dysentery, various diseases, and famine, of which peasants are often the victims. Travel is very difficult, slow, and dangerous. This is the likely reason epidemics[8] remain localized. Local lords engage in occasional warfare, looting, and pillage.

Gregory mentions wine dozens of times in his *History*. There is only one reference to cider, and none to beer. Everybody drinks wine, albeit of varying quality. Wine is a part of every day diet, as water is not safe to drink. The wealthy can afford the most delicate wines. The soldiers and the common people drink cheap wine. This aspect of wine drinking does not change over the millennia. In section III.19 of his *History*, Gregory writes that the hills west of the city of Dijon "...are covered with fruitful vines, which yield so noble a Falernum-type wine that the inhabitants have been known to scorn a good Mâcon." The reference to the Falernum indicates how highly regarded this famous Roman wine still is, some 150 years after the fall of Rome. Gregory mentions Bordeaux and its bishops but, surprisingly, not its wines.

Gregory recounts how Clovis gradually overcomes all the other lords in Frankish lands and establishes relative political stability within the country. In 507, Clovis defeats the Visigoths, thus securing his southern border. Aquitaine is now controlled by the Franks. Paris and Aachen[9] are the principal cities of the Frankish kingdom.

---

5. Hospitals and universities would later own vineyards as well. The most famous hospital-owned vineyards are those of the Hospices de Beaune in Burgundy. The University Pierre et Marie Curie in Paris still produces a delicious *vin doux naturel* from its vineyards in Banyuls-sur-mer.
6. The first monastery is established at Monte Cassino. St. Benedict is its first Abbot.
7. Gregory of Tours, *History of the Franks*, (591) translated by L. Thorpe (Penguin, 1974).
8. Gregory describes local epidemics of bubonic plague, a disease that will devastate all of Europe in the mid 1300s.
9. Aachen, in French: Aix-la-Chapelle, is in Northwest Germany.

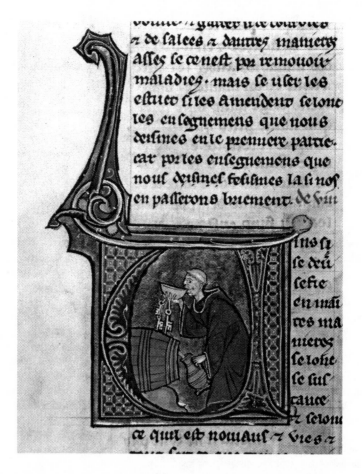

*Figure 28: The cellarer always strictly obeys the Rules of St. Benedict. Well, almost always...
From the late 13th century manuscript "Li Livres dou Santé" (The Book of Health) by Aldo-
brandino di Siena (© British Library).*

Around the year 500, the Vandals occupy the North African coast, southern Spain and much of Italy, until 533. The Visigoths dominate the Iberian Peninsula and a bit of southern France, until 711. The Ostrogoths control northern Italy, Switzerland, and Austria. The Saxons dominate eastern England. The Franks control most of France and Belgium. The Celts are established in Brittany and western England. Ireland, mostly untouched by all these events, maintains Greco-Roman and Christian traditions.

Natural disasters, famines, epidemics, and general misery mark much of the 6th century. The Vesuvius erupts again in 513, an earthquake destroys Antioch, another severely shakes Constantinople, floods ruin crops, and the great "plague of Justinian" (558-590) decimates the population. This is the first major outbreak of bubonic plague in history.[10] Within two years, it kills some 70,000 people in the city of Constantinople alone, and dooms Justinian's ambitions to reunify Imperial Rome.

The long period of instability that follows the fall of Rome greatly affects wines. The upscale Roman market for quality wines no longer exists. Amphorae are gone for good, except in Greece, southern Italy, and the Middle East. More importantly, the technical expertise of the Romans and their ability to age wines are either forgotten or cannot be implemented for lack of infrastructure. While the better Roman and Greek wines could age for years and sometimes decades, the early medieval wines never achieve such qualities. These wines are weak and acidic, mostly white or pale in color, and rarely survive as long as one year.[11] The price of a six-months-old wine is only about half that of a new one. Red wines, obtained from red grapes macerated for a long time, are rare.

In the early Middle Ages, the quality of the wine is low by today's standards. Wine presses are expensive. Only wealthy estates, large abbeys or monasteries, are well equipped. Common wine is obtained by foot-treading for a short time, which produces a light blush-type wine, with only 7 or 8% alcohol.[12] The maceration and fermentation often take place in open air, probably to prevent carbon dioxide poisoning.

The barrels, often left outdoors,[13] are not topped off to compensate for evaporation and leaks. Exposed to oxygen, the wine turns to vinegar over weeks or months. When wine is draw from a barrel, all of it contains must be drunk without much delay: "*quand le vin est tiré, il faut le boire*" (when wine is drawn [from a barrel], it must be drunk). No wine survives very long: there are no airtight amphorae or bottles in which wine can age. There is no resin from the Terebinth tree or other additives to slow down the vinegar bacteria. Wood barrels leak and wines oxidize.

No substantial technological advance takes place during this period, except that monks discover that egg whites can be used to clarify the wine. Most wine producers appear to be no less knowledgeable about winemaking than the Greeks or Romans.

Trade barriers are in place to protect the local production, which itself cannot reach distant markets for the same reason. Even the best red wines of the time, produced in Burgundy, are hard to find in Paris, while the wines from Bordeaux and the Rhône region are essentially unknown beyond their natural boundaries. There is a demand for the sweet, more powerful, and longer-lasting wines from Lebanon, Crete, or Sicily, but these are very rare and expensive. The

---

10. H. Zinsser, *Rats, Lice, and History* (Black Dog and Leventhal, New York, 1996).
11. F. Autrand, *Historia* **73**, 32 (2001).
12. Ibid.
13. Wine cellars appeared only in the late Middle Ages.

warmer climate in the south means that the grapes are fully mature at harvest: the more sugar in the must, the higher the alcohol in the wine, and the longer it survives.

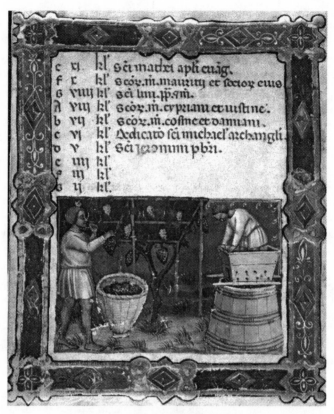

Figure 29: Treading grapes in the Middle Ages.
(Officium Beatae Virginis. Italian codex, 14th c., Biblioteca Civica, Forli, Italy. Photo: Scala, © Art Resource, NY)

Commercial rather than geological reasons dictate the location of new vineyards. They have to be near a large city or a major river, thus facilitating the sale or shipping of wines. Overland transport is difficult, slow and unsafe. Thus, the regions around Paris and near the rivers Rhine, Loire, or Rhône are favored, while Burgundy is at a disadvantage.

The region of Champagne is the spiritual center of France. This is where St. Rémi, bishop of Reims, baptizes Clovis (in 496). The kings of France will always be crowned there as well. However, the wine produced in Champagne in the early Middle Ages is nothing like the delicate bubbly we know today. Champagne is quite far north, where summers are short and winters arrive early. The grapes seldom fully mature. The wine is light, weak, acidic, and unstable.

Bordeaux wines are mostly unknown in the early Middle Ages, probably because the region is geographically isolated. The Romans had established its harbor and vineyards to ship wines to their troops in northern France and England. After the collapse of the Roman Empire, the region's wines are quickly forgotten. Their revival occurs in the 12th century.

The climate improves. The 5th and 6th centuries are cold, but they are followed by the "medieval warm epoch," which lasts until the early 1300s. This benefits agriculture, especially viticulture, throughout Europe. The population of Europe nearly doubles, from about 40 million people in the year 1000 to some 80 million in 1300. Commercial vineyards thrive as far north as the Welch border in England. The average harvest in Western Europe takes place about one month earlier than it does today.

In the 7th century, something unexpected happens: Islam. This new religion emerges from Medina and Mecca and spread like wildfire. It soon dominates a territory ranging from Afghanistan to the southern border of the Byzantine Empire (roughly southern Turkey), the entire Middle East, Egypt and North Africa, and most of the Iberian Peninsula, which the Moors control after expelling the Visigoths at Guadalete in 711. The Moors push into France but Charles Martel[14] crushes them at the battle of Poitiers in 732. However, by 800, almost half of the known world is Muslim.

Pepin the Short, son of Charles Martel, rules over a Christian kingdom from his administrative capital Aachen. His son Charlemagne, the first Holy Roman Emperor, extends and consolidates the Frankish empire.[15] At its peak, it includes much of Western Europe, from the river Elbe to Italy, France, and a touch of Spain. Charlemagne is a formidable presence and holds the Empire together in great part by the power of his reputation and personality. He encourages learning, the arts, and wines. He gives the hill of Corton to the abbey of Saulieu in 775, and demands that a white cultivar be planted there. Red wine taints his white beard... This vineyard becomes "Corton-Charlemagne." Today, it produces a most distinguished Chardonnay. During Charlemagne's reign, Abbeys and vineyards appear in Champagne.

---

14. Charles is nicknamed "Martel" (in French, *marteau* means hammer) because he badly hammered the Muslims in 732, between the cities of Poitiers and Tours.
15. A. Barbero, *Charlemagne, Father of a Continent* (University of California Press, Berkeley, 2000).

Figure 30: Corton Charlemagne: a remarkable Chardonnay (courtesy: Maison Louis Latour)

Thus, between the years 450 and 800, the western world has completely changed. The Roman Empire is a distant memory. Italy has become a weak and divided kingdom. Charlemagne controls much of Europe, the Slavs and Hungarians dominate the east, the Byzantine Empire includes the southeast and Constantinople.

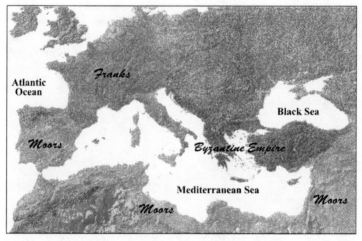

Figure 31: The key players around AD 800 (map: Kristin Reid).

Charlemagne dies in 814 and the political stability he maintained disappears. His son, the inept Louis the Pious, reigns until 840. Charlemagne's empire
is then divided among Louis' three sons. Louis the German gets the East, Charles
the Bold the West and Lothair inherits the vertical slice of Europe running from
Northern Germany to Italy. This territory has neither strong natural boundaries
nor political, linguistic, or economic unity.

It is Charles who gives land in Chablis to the Chapter of St. Martin de
Tours, in 867. The monks quickly discover that the region produces exceptional
wines. Since the river Yonne flows into the river Seine, the region also has easy
access to Paris.

In 987, Hugh Capet is elected King and moves the capital to Paris. His
dynasty, the Capetians, rule France until 1871, with interruptions during the
French revolution and the reign of Napoleon. But the first Capetians only control
a small region around Paris.

By the 9th century, some of the wines produced along the Rhine River are
shipped to England. Wines are also shipped from Bordeaux to England and
Ireland. Champagne is at the crossroads of two major trade routes: Flanders-
Italy and Paris-Rhine. Some of its wines are exported, but they are not highly
regarded. Paris is surrounded by vineyards. But a new threat to life, property,
and trade arrives from Northern Europe: the Norsemen, also known as Vikings.[16]

The first Viking raid takes place on June 8, 793, at the monastery of Saint
Catherine on the small island of Lindisfarne, off the eastern coast of England.
The monks are slaughtered and the monastery sacked. This raid is the first of
many. The Vikings terrify populations not only along the coasts of northern
Europe, but also far inland. They sail up rivers and threaten cities (and vineyards). Paris, Tours, Bordeaux, and other cities are sacked, multiple times. Some
cities offer to pay hefty ransoms but the Vikings rarely play by the rules. They
take the ransom, and then sack the city anyway. As a result a migration inland,
away from the vulnerable cities, takes place.

While the Vikings enjoy pillaging, they also trade all over Western and
Eastern Europe as well as the Middle East. This includes the wine trade. In
Ireland, the Vikings establish the city of Dublin. In the North-West, they
establish colonies in Iceland and Greenland. In the year 1000, Leif Erickson, son
of Eric the Red, reaches North America at l'Anse aux Meadows, Newfoundland.
His small community survives there for a decade or so, and then disappears. In
the East, the Vikings find their way into Russia. In the South, they establish a
powerful Norman Kingdom in Sicily. In 911, they conquer a large area in the
mouth of the river Seine, Normandy, from where William I conquers England in
1066. The Normans plant vineyards in England.

The Vikings are Christians and enjoy wine. Leif Erickson brings Christianity to Greenland and a bishop resides there. However, there is no evidence of

---

16. P. Sawyer, *The Oxford Illustrated Story of the Vikings* (Oxford University Press, 1997).

viticulture and winemaking associated with this. The Vikings have a high sense of democracy, something that is lacking elsewhere in the world at the time. Their rulers are called "first among equals." However, in much of Europe, they are remembered for pillaging, not for the finer details of their social structure.

The year 1096 marks the beginning of the Crusades. These bloody expeditions affect the history of wine in that, at their departure, some crusaders donate vineyards to monasteries in exchange for prayers and, at their return, they bring back to Europe Arab science and technology, in particular distillation.

ARAB CONTRIBUTIONS

For a number of centuries following the fall of Rome, most of Western Europe is in turmoil. The Arabs become the custodians of civilization. They translate ancient texts and further develop medicine, technology, mathematics, and astronomy. Intellectual centers thrive in the Middle East, in particular in Teheran and Damascus, as well as in Southern Spain: Toledo, Cordoba, Grenada, and Sevilla are intellectual centers. In Cordoba, Al-Zahrawi (936-1013), better known as Albucasis, writes a 30-volume medical encyclopedia and designs modern-looking surgical instruments. Many consider him the father of surgery.

Throughout the Middle Ages, new knowledge arrives in Western Europe from Islam and China. The Arabs maintain glass-blowing skills and, in the 9th century, invented distillation. Alembic (*al-anbiq*) and alcohol (*al-koh'l*) are Arabic words. Mohammad Ibn Zakariya Razi (864-930) invents, or at least perfects, the art of distillation. He is famous for his medical skills, and is the believed to be the first to use opium for anesthesia. He is also a mathematician, astronomer, philosopher, and alchemist[17] — interested in changing common metals into gold. Razi truly is an early renaissance man, long before the European Renaissance. His tomb is located in south Teheran.

Distillation arrives in the West in the 12th century with Crusaders returning from the Middle East. Nearly pure alcohol first appears in Italy and quickly gains importance for its medicinal value as an antiseptic. Nothing more powerful is available until penicillin.[18] Alcohol also serves as an additive to strengthen wine and stabilize it during transport by sea. But distillation also leads to alcoholism.

---

17. The words "alchemy" and "chemistry" come from "kimia," literally "precious" as in gold.
18. Sir Alexander Fleming (1881-1955) discovers penicillin in 1928. It is first mass-produced during World War II.

Figure 32: August 27 is Pharmacy Day or "Razi Day" in Iran. The date in Arabic on the stamp, 2537, refers to Cyrus the Great.[19] The accent is misplaced on "Journeé" ("Journée" (photo SKE).

The distillation of wine is based on the difference in the evaporation temperature of water (212°F) and alcohol (172°F). One evaporates then condenses the alcohol from wine. In order to obtain nearly pure alcohol, several distillations are required.

Alcohol is referred to as *quintessence*, literally the "fifth element" — something important enough to rank with air, water, fire, and earth. In Germany, it is called *gebrandtewein* ("burnt wine"), and this becomes the Dutch *brandewijn*, the origin of "brandy." In France, the region of Armagnac becomes an importance center of distillation in the 1300s (Cognac emerges some three centuries later). High-quality alcohol from the wine produced in the soil of Armagnac is obtained after just one or two distillations.

The Qur'an contains the earliest language limiting or even outright banning the consumption of alcohol. It mentions wine or drinking seven times. Only two verses contain strict language against its consumption, while one of them (Surah 47.15, quoted in the first chapter) promises to the believers "rivers of wine" in the gardens of heaven.

Surah 2.21 offers:
They question thee about strong drinks and games of chance.
Say: in both is great sin and (some) utility for men; but the sin of them is greater than their usefulness...

---

19. In 1971, the Shah of Iran celebrates the 2,500 anniversary of the capture of Babylon by Cyrus the Great, which marks the beginning of the Persian Empire. Thus, he sets 529 BCE as year zero of the Iranian calendar during his reign. However, history books place the capture of Babylon at 539 BCE. The Zoroastrian calendar works in mysterious ways.

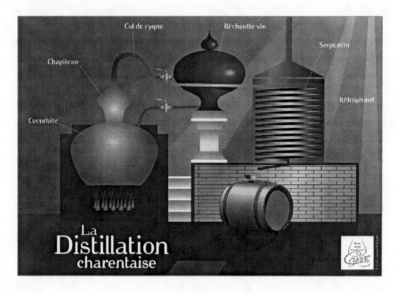

Figures 33-34: Modern alembic in Cognac: the pre-heated wine (bulb-like container at center) evaporates into the boiler (left). The vapors, mostly alcohol, are sent through a water-cooled spiral (right) and drip into the barrel. (Courtesy: Bureau National Interprofessionnel du Cognac; photo: Gérard Martron)

Surah 4.43
O ye who believe! Draw not near unto prayer when ye are drunken,
till ye know that which ye utter, not when ye are polluted
save when journeying upon the road, till ye have bathed...

Surah 5.90
O ye who believe! Strong drink and games of chance and idols and divining arrows
are only an infamy of Satan's handiwork. Leave it aside in order that ye may succeed.

Surah 5.91
Satan seeketh only to cast among your enmity and hatred by means of strong drink and
games of chances,
and to turn you from remembrance of Allah and from worship.

Surah 16.67
And of the fruits of the date-palm, and grapes, whence ye derive strong drink and (also)
good nourishment.
Lo! herein is indeed a portent for people who reflect.

Surah 83.25
They are given to drink pure wine, sealed.

The word used is often *khamr*, wine from grapes. In the Hadith[20] literature, the second Caliph writes: "[wine] comes from five kinds of fruit: grapes, dates, honey, wheat, and barley. Wine is what obscures the intellect." Endless interpretations followed about the letter and the spirit of the law. Wine remains tolerated in medicine.

The prohibition is variously enforced. Over the centuries, the production and use of wine continues in Islamic countries. The Maliki jurist Ibn Abdun offers legal opinions regarding Jews and Christians in Seville around 1100: "a drunken man should only be whipped after he becomes sober."

Recipes suggest how to mix wine and water, typically, 1/3 wine with 2/3 water. The Moors encourage the production of wines by non-Muslims and tax the product. Sometimes, they even enjoy wine themselves. Viticulture survives in a few Muslim countries. The most celebrated wine from the Near East is probably Chateau Musar, just outside of Beirut in Lebanon. The grapes grow in the Bekaa Valley. But wines are also produced in Algeria, Egypt, Jordan, and other countries, even near the city of Shiraz in Iran — albeit unofficially. Arak — an alcohol often distilled from wine and flavored with anis seeds — is widely

---

20. The Traditions (*Hadith* in Arabic) are the collected sayings and acts attributed to the Prophet.

available. Other countries, such as Saudi Arabia, strictly enforce the ban on alcohol production and consumption.

*Figures 35-36: Above,
an Egyptian wine from the Karm Al Nada estate
(courtesy A. Hadji-Thomas) and right,
a Jordanian Arak (photo SKE).*

There are many references to wine and drinking in the Arab literature, such as in the poems of Abu Nuwas (757-815) or the Comments of Judah ben Solomon Harizi (1170-1235): "[wine is] an unreliable emissary: I sent it down to my stomach, and it went up to my head." Omar Khayyam, the famous 12th century Persian poet and scientist, often mentions wines and drinking, as in,[21]

*Yesterday this Day's Madness did prepare;
Tomorrow's Silence, Triumph or Despair:
Drink! For you know not whence you came nor why:
Drink! For you know not why you go nor where.*

---

21. E. Fitzgerald, *The Rubáiyát of Omar Khayyám*, fifth ed., number 74 (Dover, 1990).

EMERGENCE OF BURGUNDY AND BORDEAUX

Overview

The quality of wines and the opportunities associated with the wine trade gradually increase during the second half of the Middle Ages and several key wine-producing regions of France emerge. This begins in the late 11th century in Burgundy, because of independent and hard-working monks. Then, the region of Bordeaux returns on the wine scene, an unforeseen consequence of the marriage of Eleanor of Aquitaine to the future King Henry II of England. Côtes du Rhône comes next, as the Papacy moves from Rome to Avignon in the early 14th century. Popes demand luxury, including good wine, and new vineyards are planted. Burgundy, Bordeaux and, to a lesser extent, Côtes du Rhône acquire a reputation of excellence that continues today. This is not to say that these are the only wine regions. In fact, around the year 1000, wine is produced almost everywhere in Europe and around the Mediterranean basin. However, in the Iberian Peninsula, North Africa, and the near East, Islam limits, and at places prohibits, its production and trade. Italy and much of central Europe are divided and politically weak. The wine production remains local. Thus, as far as wines with a reputation of quality are concerned, Burgundy and Bordeaux have little competition, and their reputation will remain for centuries. In the 1300s, a major climatic change in Europe, the "Little Ice Age," followed by the first waves of Black Plague, shake the social structure to its core, mark the beginning of the end of feudality, and change the geographical distribution of vineyards. The first Golden Age of Burgundy occurs under the reign of four powerful Dukes.

Cistercian wines

Until the 11th century, all bishops are appointed by the king, a principle imposed by Charlemagne. Pope Leon IX (1049-1054) and his successor Gregory VII (1020?-1085) initiate a policy of emancipation from the temporal power. In 1075, Gregory decrees that only the Pontiff of Rome can be called Universal. Only he can appoint and depose bishops. Further, since the Pope crowns kings and emperors, he can also depose them. Excommunication is his weapon: an excommunicated ruler loses legitimacy. But monasteries also fit in the secular feudal system. Kings, dukes, or other powerful rulers establish them, give them land, and then appoint their abbots. This is also about to change.

In 909, William, Duke of Aquitaine and the monk Berno establish a Benedictine monastery at Cluny, near the city of Mâcon in Burgundy, which benefits from a "pontifical exemption." This means that it is under the direct authority of the pope, free from secular obligations. The influence and power of Cluny rapidly grows. In order to counteract the influence of the Benedictines (who wear black habits), Cistercian[22] monks (who wear white habits) establish the monasteries of Molesme (1075) then Cîteaux (1098), just east of Nuits-St.-George, also in Burgundy. They follow the same rules, those of St. Benedict, but apply them to the letter, with principles of penitence. They are also under the direct authority of the pope. These independent monasteries encourage reform within the Church. Monastic life — pray, work, rest — quickly becomes popular. The appeal of religious life increases. One reason is the new fervor associated with the Crusades. Another reason is the insecurity of cities caused by frequent Vikings raids. Yet another reason is that monastic life is overall safer than life in cities or small rural communities.

As the population of an abbey outgrows its capacity, a group of monks leaves and establishes a new abbey elsewhere. The number of Cistercian abbeys[23] grows enormously until the onset of the Little Ice Age in the early 1300s. This begins with the daughter-abbeys of Cîteaux, Pontigny, Clairvaux, and Morimond. From a handful in 1100, the number of Cistercian abbeys grows to about 300 in 1150, 500 in 1200, 650 in 1250, and 697 in 1300. These numbers exclude hundreds of nunneries. Cistercian abbeys are built from Portugal to Russia and from Sicily to Scotland. Most of them are impressive structures, with magnificent churches, buildings, and fantastic cellars for keeping wine, the first extensive wine cellars.

The Cistercians are quality fanatics. They have plenty of time, manpower and financial resources. In Burgundy, it is claimed that they even taste soil samples before deciding where to plant new vineyards. They bring the Chardonnay grape to region of Chablis. They introduce the notions of terroir and cru.[24] "Terroir" refers to the soil, exposure, slope, and other physical characteristics of a vineyard. "Cru" relates a wine to the grapes that grow in a specific geographical location. The Cistercians vastly improve winemaking techniques, mostly by systematic trial and error. This extends from the pruning of vines to winemaking techniques. The quality of the wines they produce in Burgundy, including red wines, increases substantially. Cistercian wines are far better than those produced elsewhere at the time.

---

22. "Cistercian" originates from the French *cistelle*, a reed prevalent in the region where the monastery of Cîteaux, originally "Cisteaux," was built. In French, the modern "î" and "ô" often replace the ancient "is" and "os."

23. J.F. Leroux-Dhuys and H. Gaud, *Cistercian Abbey: history and architecture* (Könemann, Cologne, 1988).

24. *Terroir* comes from the French *terre*, the earth or dirt in which the vine grows. *Cru* comes from the verb *croître*, to grow.

Figure 37: St. John's College at Oxford University, established in 1555, is built on much older Cistercian foundations. The cellars are well-stocked (photo SKE)

Revival of Bordeaux

The wines from the region of Bordeaux are hardly ever mentioned in the early Middle Ages. While viticulture certainly continues there after Roman times, these wines no longer have a market. Bordeaux is geographically isolated. The Romans established the harbor and planted the vineyards in order to provide wine for their legions in England, not for trade within continental Europe. After the Romans armies leave England and northern France, this market disappears and the wines from Bordeaux have nowhere to go. This situation changes when Eleanor of Aquitaine[25] (1122-1204), one of the most remarkable and powerful women in all of history, arrives on the scene.

In the 11th century, the duchy of Aquitaine is much larger than the lands directly under the control of the King of France. Indeed, Louis VI (1108-1137) initially owns only Paris and St. Denis. However, he has a long-term vision for the kingdom. In 1137, he arranges for his son Louis (soon to be Louis VII) to marry the young and beautiful Eleanor, heiress of Aquitaine. They have two daughters,

25. A. Weir, *A Life: Eleanor of Aquitaine* (Ballantine, New York, 1999); M. Meade, *Eleanor of Aquitaine, a Biography* (Penguin, New York, 1991); D. Seward, *Eleanor of Aquitaine, the Mother Queen* (Dorset, New York, 1978).

Alice and Marie. However Louis has neither the stature nor the ambitions of Eleanor. Following a crusade to the Middle East, Louis became increasingly reclusive and boring. On March 21, 1152, the marriage is annulled on a technicality. On May 18 of the same year, Eleanor marries the fiery Henry Plantagenet of Anjou, who becomes Henry II of England[26] in 1154. This adds the region of Aquitaine, including Bordeaux, to the crown of England. Suddenly, England is again a market for Bordeaux wines.

Eleanor and Henry have five sons and three daughters. The most famous of these children is Richard the Lionheart. Many of Eleanor's children, grandchildren, or in-laws, become kings or queens. Later in her life Eleanor is a major behind-the-scenes player in European politics. The tombs of Eleanor, Henry II and Richard the Lionheart are at the Abbey of Fontervault, along the Loire River in France.

There are many tensions between the crowns of England and France. For one thing, Henry II has a considerable amount of land in France, and therefore is the vassal of the King of France. He is not very good at being anybody's vassal. The territorial disputes initiated with Eleanor's wedding to Henry will contribute to the Hundred Years War (1337-1453) between France and England. Bordeaux and its wines remain under English control for three centuries, until the battle of Castillon (1453), which leaves England no longer in control of French territory.

◉ The wine trade between Bordeaux and England increased enormously from 1154 to 1452. It increases slowly at first. Eleanor herself does not care much about the wine trade. But the market with England opens up when her son John becomes King. Then, a major boost occurs in 1226, when Louis IX of France takes La Rochelle, the most important port on the Atlantic. Soon afterwards, Bordeaux becomes the largest port. At their peak in the early 1300s, Bordeaux shipments of wine to England exceed 22 million gallons[27] per year. 250,000 gallons of wine are consumed during the coronation of Edward II. A planting frenzy accompanies the increase in the wine trade, and the city grows substantially. The wine trade with Bordeaux is so large that the capacity of ships is measured by the number of barrels they can carry. The wines are shipped in "tuns," large casks of about 950 liters. The French *tonneau* comes from the medival *tun*.

In the 1300s, the English drink more Bordeaux wine than they do today, with only 5% of today's population. They called it "claret." The word "claret"

---

26. William of Normandy becomes William I of England following the battle of Hastings. The reigns of William Rufus (1089-1099) and Henry I (1100-1135) are followed by a civil war involving Henry's daughter Mathilda and Stephen, who usurps the crown. Mathilda's son Henry is Eleanor's second husband. He becomes the powerful Henry II in 1154.

27. T. Brennan, *Burgundy to Champagne: the Wine Trade in Early Modern France* (Johns Hopkins, Baltimore, 1997).

probably relates to the light color, *clair* in French, of the Bordeaux wines from that period. Red and white grapes are pressed and fermented together, producing light-colored wines which contrast with the much darker wines produced in northern Spain. The first long-macerated, barrel-matured, deep-red Bordeaux wines are produced much later, in the late 1600s, by the Pontac family at Haut-Brion.

ONSET OF THE LITTLE ICE AGE

A sudden and dramatic climatic change, the Little Ice Age,[28] affects Europe in the early 1300s. The cool-down first hits Greenland and Iceland. The Vikings settlements in Greenland disappear. In continental Europe, the Little Ice Age begins with the very cold winter of 1309/10. Incessant rains start late spring 1315, and hardly stop for three years. The few crops that manage to grow never mature; the food supplies rot; the top soil erodes away. Vines are attacked by mildew and wine becomes scarce. Domestic animals starve or are eaten. A three-year long famine devastates the continent. Tens of thousands starve in central and northern Europe. The harsh winters of 1317-8 and 1322-3 compound the misery.

Unpredictable weather lasts for centuries, with occasional warm summers and many bitterly cold periods. Very cold winters are recorded in the 1430s, resulting again in widespread famine (1433-1438). In the 1450s, viticulture is mostly abandoned in England.[29] Very cold winters in the late 1780s contribute to bread riots in Paris. The "official" end of the Little Ice Age coincides with the Irish potato famine in the mid-1850s.

The details of weather fluctuations in Europe at the time are somewhat sketchy. Well-calibrated climatic data exist for only a few locations.[30] Such data come from tree rings, ice cores, historical accounts, logbooks of ships, accounts of wine harvests, and similar sources. Such records are not available everywhere and for all periods. However, reasonable data in Europe provide a rather good picture of the average climate[31] in central and northern Europe for much of Antiquity and the Middle Ages.

---

28. B. Fagan, *The Little Ice Age* (Basic Books, New York, 2000).
29. Viticulture has resumed in Southern England in the past decade or so. However, English wines are mentioned in the 1600s by Samuel Pepys, in his Diary, indicating that at least a few vineyards remain productive.
30. R.S. Bradley, M.K. Hughes, and H.F. Diaz, Science **302**, 404 (2003).
31. See R.H. Dott, Jr. and D.R. Prothero, *Evolution of the Earth* (McGraw Hill, 1994), and the National Oceanic and Atmospheric Administration, at *www.ngdc.noaa.gov/paleo/ctl/index.html* as well as *www.aip.prg/history/climate*. For the past 500 years, see J. Luterbacher *et al.*, Science **303**, 1499 (2004).

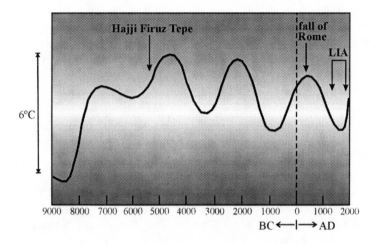

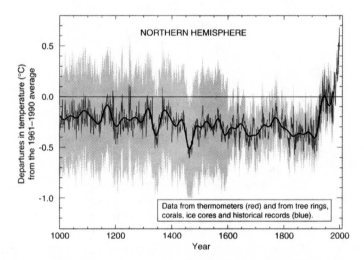

Figures 38-39: Average temperature fluctuations in the Northern Hemisphere. Top, long-term estimates back to the last major Ice Age. "LIA" is the Little Ice Age (drawing: Kristin Reid). Below, compilation of data from tree rings, corals, ice cores and historical records. Data after the mid-1800s include thermometer readings and show a warming trend (courtesy Michael E. Mann, Pennsylvania State University). Note that the vertical scale in the upper figure is about five times larger than the one in the lower figure.

Following the climatic change, waves of Black Plague hit Europe with a vengeance. The first wave starts in 1347 in Messina, Sicily, when a ship from the Middle East arrives with most of its crew dead or dying. Carried by rat fleas, the plague spreads fast. About one-third of the population of Europe dies between

1348 and 1350. Other waves of plague sweep Europe in 1361, 1371 and 1382. These are much less devastating because the survivors of the original outbreak and their descendents develop some immunity to the disease. However, further outbreaks continue until the 17th century.

The feudal structure is shaken to its core. The medieval system of agriculture is labor-intensive, and the succession of famines and plagues leads to a severe lack of manpower in many places. The population of serfs, those virtual slaves attached to a piece of land, sharply drops. Labor is scarce, and it becomes increasingly hard to enforce serfdom. In order to boost their populations, cities such as Tours offer freedom to serfs who avoid capture by their landlords for a year and a day.

OTHER WINE REGIONS

The corrupt papacy in the early 1300s is very unpopular in Rome. Many nobles refuse to pay papal taxes and provide military service. In Rome itself, mass riots take place. Further, serious challenges to the power of the pope come from France. King Phillip IV (reigns 1285-1314) and Pope Boniface VIII (1294-1303) clash over taxation and secular vs. canon law. This goes as far as Boniface being arrested and jailed. The Pope is released but dies soon after. Then, a French cardinal is elected pope in 1305: Clement V. He moves the papacy to the city of Avignon in Southern Côtes du Rhône. The Popes remain there until 1378. These Popes enjoy lavish lifestyles, sumptuous palaces, delicate foods, quality wines, and all the comforts this life provides. It is not too surprising that their arrival in Avignon coincides with the reappearance of quality wines in Côtes du Rhône. The vineyards of *Château-Neuf-du-Pape* are planted. Yet, these are troubled times. The Hundred Years war is ravaging large parts of the country, and the Black Death decimates millions. The Popes do very little to alleviate the suffering, and the Church loses moral authority. When Gregory XI dies in Rome in 1378, a mob forces the cardinals to elect an Italian pope: Urban VI is elected and promises to stay in Rome. But the French cardinals declare the election invalid and select their own pope, whose papacy is in Avignon. At the council of Pisa in 1408, the cardinals depose both popes and elect a new one. However, cardinals have no standing in deposing popes; there are now three popes... The madness ends in 1415.

The Avignon Popes Clement V and John XXII are also very fond of the monastic wines from the region of Beaune. These wines are transported at great expense from Burgundy to Avignon. This trade increases the awareness and reputation of Burgundy wines throughout Europe.

Ø Champagne wines play a minor role in the late Middle Ages. In the mid 1300s, Champagne is as far north as wine can still be cultivated. The summers are short, late spring and early fall freezes common. The grapes have enough sugar to make wine with sufficient alcohol content only in the warmest summers.

Further, the alcoholic fermentation is rarely finished in the fall by the time the temperature drops and the yeast goes dormant with the onset of winter. The following spring, the yeast awakens and fermentation resumes, causing unwanted bubbles of carbon dioxide in the wine. Finally, the malolactic fermentation rarely occurs. This fermentation, caused by bacteria, transforms the harsh malic acid into the softer lactic acid, which reduces the acidity in the wine. As a result, the wine from Champagne tends to be light (low in alcohol content), acidic, and a little bubbly. These are all considered to be signs of poor quality. However, the production is large and, in the early 1400s, the wine trade is an important business in Reims.

In medieval Italy, as in Roman times, everyday diet is based on bread, olives, and wine. The trade is limited because the country is politically divided and transportation difficult. The impact of the Little Ice Age is much weaker south than north of the Alps. Between the 11th and 14th centuries, the population increases from 5 to some 8 million people, and urban centers grow. The merchant cities of Genova and Venice become rich and powerful. The bankers of Florence, such as the Antinori, go into the wine business. By the 14th century, many of today's most important vineyards are planted with the cultivars we know today: Barbera, Nebbiolo, Sangiovese ... The reputation of Italian wines, in particular from Tuscany, grows. Chianti is first mentioned in 1398. This wine is a blend of cultivars, mostly Sangiovese, but also Camaiolo, Malvasia, Trebbiano, and others, all of which grow in the same vineyard and are harvested, pressed, and fermented together.

Venice gains a quasi-monopoly on the trade with the Orient, including the intense sweet wines from Lebanon and Cyprus. However, by the second half of the 15th century the power of Venice diminishes as the center of influence shifts from the East to the West. The ramifications of this shift are sometimes dramatic, such as the explorations of the African coast or the discovery of America, and sometimes subtle, such as the move of the Hospitaller knights from Cyprus to Rhodes. In Cyprus, they make a famous dessert wine, the *Commandaria*, still produced there today.

In Spain, the Moorish influence is fading. By 1300, only Granada remains Moorish. In 1469, Ferdinand of Aragon marries Isabella of Castile, thus unifying most of Spain under their dual crowns. They set to complete the expulsion of the Moors from Spain. On January 1, 1492, Boabdil, the last ruler of Moorish *Al-Andalus* surrenders the keys of Granada.

The Catholic fervor of Ferdinand and (especially) Isabella leads to the ruthless Spanish Inquisition, and the expulsion of not only Muslims, but also Jews, and later Protestants. The first new mosque in Granada in 500 years is built in the summer of 2003. Ironically, it is next to the *Convento de las Tomasas*. The Sisters are said to be less than thrilled by the calls to Muslim prayer, starting at 5:30am.

The wines produced in Spain at the end of the Middle Ages are for the most part of low quality. The wine is sometimes mixed with honey to increase its appeal and longevity. Powerful deep reds, known as "black wines," are made in the north, along the banks of the river Duero. These wines are of much higher quality. Strong and dry wines are also produced in the South, near Jerez and Cadix. These ancestors of the sherry, not yet fortified, are exported to England where they are called *sack*.

Portugal gains independence from the Moors in the mid-12th century but its trade with England is limited.[32] A key event is the capture of Lisbon from the Moors in October, 1147, following a four-month siege.[33] This siege involves crusaders from Northern Europe on their way (by ship) to the Middle East. They stop to help King Alfonso Henriques of Portugal (1139-1185) capture Lisbon. The wines produced in the Upper Douro valley, where today's Ports are made, are still a local and rather poor-quality product. These wines will emerge as Ports more than a century after the arrival of the English, who lose Bordeaux at the end of the Hundred Years War.

In Central and Eastern Europe, the area dedicated to viticulture and the wine production grow throughout the Medieval Warm Epoch. In some regions, such as the east coast of the Adriatic and parts of today's Bulgaria, Romania, Moldova, and Ukraine (Crimean peninsula), viticulture dates back to the days of Ancient Greece. In other regions, the first vineyards are believed to have been planted in Roman times, such as in parts of today's Czech Republic (Moravia), Austria or Hungary. Many vineyards survive the invasions from the East and the fall of Rome.

In the 9th century, it is reported that Bulgarian monks keep their wines in deep cellars. By the10th century, the sweet wines produced in Halkidiki (Macedonia) are sold throughout Greece and even exported to Constantinople.

Numerous new vineyards are planted during the late Middle Ages until the early 1300s. Following the onset of the Little Ice Age, the wine production drops and many vineyards are abandoned.

THE FIRST GOLDEN AGE OF BURGUNDY

The first Golden Age of Burgundy lasts from 1364 to 1477, owing to four powerful and wine-loving dukes. At its height, Burgundy includes much of northern France, Belgium, Luxemburg, and the Netherlands, a size that makes it a threat to the king of France. The arts prosper, the monastic orders grow, and the emphasis on wine quality rather than quantity is enforced.

---

32. The friendship between Portugal and England, sealed at the Treaty of Windsor in 1386, still lasts today.

33. C. Tyerman, *The Crusades, A Very Short Introduction* (Oxford UP, Oxford, 2004).

The first duke is Philip the Bold (1342-1404). In 1395, he orders[34] the prolific but common Gamay cultivar pulled from the region and replaced by the
Pinot Noir: No Gamay grows in Burgundy[35] proper since then. These are the first
official regulations limiting which cultivars are allowed and forbidden in a specific geographical area. These rules survive to this day throughout France, a
legacy of Philip the Bold.

Philip is succeeded by John the Fearless (1371-1419), then Philip the Good
(1396-1467). The latter is not good to everybody. Indeed, he is the one who captures Joan of Arc and delivers her to the English, who burn her at the stake for
heresy in 1431. However, we will remember him for declaring the flat lands
around Dijon, just north of Burgundy proper, off-limits to the Pinot Noir. None
grows there still today.

In 1443 Philip's Chancellor, Nicolas Rolin, builds a public hospital for the
poor in the city of Beaune. The goal is to relieve some of the misery caused by the
Hundred Years' War. The first patient is admitted on January 1, 1453. Today, the
Hospices de Beaune still provides free care to the locals and is famous for its
wine auctions.

The last of the four great Dukes of Burgundy is the impulsive and ambitious
Charles the Bold (1433-1477). He runs into a problem: the miserable-looking but
dangerously smart Louis XI, the "Spider" King of France. Worried about the
power of Burgundy, Louis manipulates Charles into fighting the Swiss, who are
pretty tough at the time. Charles loses two important battles and is killed before
the walls of Nancy. Burgundy never again challenges the power of the King.

The winds of change, blowing this time northward from Italy, are just
beginning to be felt in the late 14th century. The Renaissance has started. This does
not involve just the arts. It is an awakening, a new way to look at the world, to
observe and study nature; it is a sudden curiosity in all human endeavors. It leads to
Gutenberg's invention of movable type, which substantially accelerates printing.
Bibles become available to the public. People can read and interpret for themselves.
The curiosity extends to navigation and the desire to explore new lands. This leads
to *v. vinifera* spreading all around the globe. Finally, the curiosity includes science
and technology. This leads to the scientific method, and ultimately to the understanding of fermentation. Winemaking is about to become a science.

---

34. His order is reissued by the Congress of winegrowers of Dijon in 1845.
35. Gamay is *the* cultivar in the region of Beaujolais, which is technically a part of
    Burgundy, albeit some 60 miles south of Burgundy proper.

Figures 40-41: Dukes of Burgundy: Philip the Bold (left, unknown painter, photo: François Jay) and Philip the Good (right, workshop of Roger van der Weyden, photo: Hugo Maertens) (© musée des Beaux Arts, Dijon, France)

CHAPTER 4. FROM THE RENAISSANCE TO WORLD WAR II: EUROPE

Wine is sunlight held together by water.
—Galileo Galilei (1564-1642)

OVERVIEW

The second half of the 15th century marks the beginning of a new era in the history of Western civilization. Leonardo da Vinci is born in 1452. The Renaissance, alive in Italy for a century, is about to explode throughout Europe. In 1453, Constantinople falls to the Turks, and Bordeaux to the French. The former marks the end of the Eastern Roman Empire. The latter marks the end of the Hundred Years' War and England's control over Bordeaux and its wines. One consequence is the increase in the English wine trade with Spain and Portugal. The trade with Spain has a few ups and many downs, but the friendship between England and Portugal is long-lasting.

In 1455, Gutenberg prints the Bible, and Martin Luther is born in 1483. The Moors are kicked out of their last bastion in Spain, Granada, in 1492. In the 1400s much of the Spanish trade, including the wine trade, is in the hands of Sephardic Jews. Following the capture of Grenada, Spain expels all those who refuse to convert to Catholicism. Most of them flee. Then, English merchants move to Spain and fill the trade vacuum. They establish basic quality controls for wine production. Ironically, many of the Jews expelled from Spain go to England, France and the Netherlands, where they return to the wine trade, often with Spain. Religious intolerance is growing throughout Europe. It explodes in the 1500s. The major wine-related event of this period is the arrival of *v. vinifera* in Central America, from where it spreads throughout the continent. This is discussed in the next chapter.

In the 1600s, the Dutch emerge as a major trading power. The first fortified wines are made, and the benefits of the noble rot are discovered. In England, the first thick and sturdy bottles are made, corks and corkscrews are perfected. In France, the monarchy becomes stronger and the power of the Church diminishes. This affects mostly the wine regions of Burgundy and Champagne, where most vineyards have been planted by monks on church property during the Middle Ages. These vineyards are now bought by the new bourgeoisie of Dijon. In Champagne, Pierre Dom Pérignon makes quality still wines. Observational science had its first major hero in Italy, Galileo Galilei. The first brand-name wines of modern times are sold and the reputation of Bordeaux is consolidated. Fermentation, the most important process in winemaking, is studied and partly understood.

The 1700s see wars and revolutions. Technology improves for ports, champagnes, and Bordeaux wines. A cataclysmic period for wine begins in the mid-1800s and lasts for over a century. It begins with natural disasters: powdery mildew, phylloxera, and downy mildew decimate the vineyards. Then, man-made disasters arrive: World War I, Prohibition, the Great Depression, and World War II.

THE 1500S: SEEDS OF CHANGE

In 1517, Martin Luther nails 95 theses to the door of Wittenberg castle church. In them, he questions the sale of "indulgences": payments to the Church for the forgiveness of sins, a practice heavily promoted by Pope Leo X, a greedy Medici. At the time, the nailing of arguments to a church door is done routinely to generate debate over specific issues. However, amateur print shops are now common in many cities, including Wittenberg. Someone prints Luther's theses; his arguments spread like wildfire, and strike a sensitive nerve. The Reformation begins before Luther himself realizes what is happening.

Pope Leo X excommunicates Luther in 1521, but it is too late. Protestantism is born. It subdivides rapidly into Anabaptism, Anglicanism, Calvinism, Lutheranism, Zwinglianism, just to name a few. The leaders of the new religions tend to tolerate the drinking of wine and beer, but insist on moderation. Drunkenness is punished. Its power threatened, the Roman Catholic Church invigorates the holy inquisition. The Counter Reformation begins. Everyone believes God is on their side. Religious wars rage across central and northern Europe from 1545 to 1650. The strongly Catholic Italy, Spain, and Portugal are less affected.

Figure 42: The imposing castle Church in Wittenberg (photo SKE).

One of the most intolerant religious leaders is John Calvin (1509-1564). He rules Geneva with an iron fist, and even has a child executed for hitting his father. Calvin closes bars and imposes his righteous views on everybody. Yet a significant part of his salary is paid in wine: 500 muids[1] per year. Rumors are that Calvin also brews his own beer.

Figure 43: The Calvinus white beer is brewed in Geneva. (courtesy: Les Frères Papinot, Geneva)

In France, thousands of Huguenots — as the French Protestants are called since about 1560 — are massacred on St. Bartholomew's Day (August 24) 1572. The civil war rages until Henry of Navarre (1553-1610), born a Huguenot, converts to Catholicism and, in 1589, becomes France's Henry IV: *Paris vaut bien une messe!* (Paris is well worth one mass) he claims. On April 13, 1598 ("Edict of Nantes"), he grants rights to Protestants in a mostly Catholic France, and creates 100 "places of safety" such as the city of La Rochelle. This halts the religious wars. This edict is revoked by Louis XIV on October 18, 1685. Fearing for their lives, large numbers of Huguenots flee France toward other protestant European countries as well as the Americas and South Africa. Many bring with them vines and wine-making skills.

---

1. The "muid" is an old Dutch unit of volume, equivalent to 3 bushels. There have been numerous definitions of the bushel, but it could be as much as 8 imperial gallons, and then one muid is 109 liters.

In the 1500s, England dominates the wine trade. Following the end of the Hundred Years War with France, the English merchants look for new suppliers of wine to make up for the clarets from Bordeaux. The English already do business in northern Portugal, where the light and fruity Vinho Verde is made. This type of wine does not travel well, and is too light for the colder and rainy climate in England. The merchants venture further south, sail as far up the Douro River as possible, and discover the deep red wines from the Upper Douro valley of Portugal. These wines make their way to England, sometimes via the fishing waters off Newfoundland, where cod is plentiful.[2]

The wines from the Upper Douro valley are unsophisticated. There are no trees in the region, and hence no barrels. The first bottles appear only in the 1600s. The grapes, with stems, are treaded by foot in stone vats (*lagares*) and the free-run juice ferments in goatskins. The English merchants often add some brandy to the wine before shipping in order to stabilize it, and mask the off-flavors. Wines with high alcohol content are sought after because they keep much longer than light wines. They are often drunk mixed with water.[3]

At that time, the wines from Northern Spain are better than those produced anywhere in Portugal. But the relations between England and Spain are stormy. They turn very sour in 1533, when Henry VIII divorces his first wife, Catherine of Aragon, the youngest surviving child of Ferdinand and Isabella of Spain. Then, matters improve, until Sir Francis Drake captures the Spanish fleet off the Isthmus of Panama in 1572. Fifteen years later, he attacks the city of Cadiz in Southern Spain, seizes 2,900 pipes of sherry and brings them to England. This turns out to be a blessing in disguise, as sherry becomes very popular in England. A new and lucrative sherry market emerges.

In 1588, King Philip II of Spain sends a huge fleet against Anglican England to capture the country and, so he hopes, convert it back to Catholicism. But the Great Armada sails just as one of the coldest decades of the Little Ice Age begins. His fleet runs into all sorts of problems, including the English fleet and violent storms which force it to sail all around England, Scotland, and Ireland before finally returning to Spain. Half the 130 ships and twenty to thirty thousand men are lost. Of those, only 1,500 die in battle. This failed expedition cripples Spain as a seafaring power. Philip II dies in 1598, leaving Spain riddled with debts, and no longer a major world power.

In Eastern Europe, the Hungarian *Tokaji* is first mentioned at the end of the 15th century. It is a dry wine at that time. The region falls under Muslim rule after the Turks, under Suleiman I, defeat Louis II at the battle of Mohàcs in 1526.

---

2. M. Kurlansky, *Cod* (Penguin, 1997).
3. Distilled wine is produced in many regions where grapes grow. This brandy is often added to barrels of drinking water onboard ships, which kills bacteria. Following the battle of Trafalgar, the body of Admiral Nelson is preserved in brandy for the voyage back to England.

The Turks dominate the region for 160 years. Wine making and drinking is tolerated but not encouraged. This is not an auspicious start for the wine that would become the dessert wine Tokaji Aszú.

THE 1600s: AN AGE OF "FIRSTS"

From 1618 to 1648, the Thirty Years' War between Catholics and Protestants ravages the Rhineland. This bloody war sees armies wandering through the countryside, looting and killing. The soldiers often bring with them diseases such as cholera, the plague, typhus and typhoid fever, which further decimate local populations. Vineyards are abandoned as cellars are continuously looted, and vineyards and winemaking equipment destroyed. This is particularly true in the region of Alsace, which suffers greatly during this period. By the end of the war, the Germans are left with so little wine that beer becomes their everyday drink. It still is today. Much of the infrastructure required to make wine must be rebuilt and many vineyards replanted. The new cultivar of choice is the Riesling, Germany's most popular grape today.

A number of "firsts" occur in the 1600s: the first brand-name wine of modern times, that is, a wine sold as the product of a specific estate; the encouragement of fortification of wines by the Dutch; the production of late-harvest wines; and the use of sulphur to "clean" wine barrels before they are filled. Dom Pérignon produces the first quality (still) white wines in Champagne; the first sturdy glass bottles are manufactured; the first noble-rot wine is made. This adds up to a remarkable century for wine.

The first brand-name wine

In the 17th century, Londoners[4] do not drink water or milk. The River Thames is polluted and, without refrigeration or pasteurization, milk turns sour quickly. Tea is a novelty. Coffee is more widely available but only at specialized Coffee Houses, and it is expensive. The diarist Samuel Pepys (1633-1703) normally drinks light beer for breakfast, and beer or wine with meals.[5] Drinking rather large amounts of mildly alcoholic beverages seems to be the norm. Dozens of wines are commonly available in London. They have generic names such as "Claret," "French," "Florence," "burnt," "mulled," "sack" — sherry or Spanish white wine — or simply "red" or "white." However, on April 10, 1663, Pepys

---

4. Safe drinking water is not available anywhere, a particularly serious problem in large cities.
5. Pepys mentions numerous wines throughout his diary, including Champagne, the popular sweet wines from the Canary Islands, as well as English wines. Pepys himself has an extensive wine cellar.

records:[6] "[at the] Royall Oake Taverne in Lumbard-street, I drank a sort of French wine called Ho Bryan that hath a good and most perticular taste that I never met with." This is of course Château Haut-Brion, the first recorded brand-name wine since Roman times. Pepys' mention of this wine comes two years before Arnaud de Pontac, the owner of Château Haut-Brion, opens an upscale tavern in London from where he distributes his wines, the famed "Pontac's Head."

Figure 44: A wine screw-press dated 1669 at the Frederic Mochel winery in Traenheim, Alsace (photo SKE).

Samuel Pepys later becomes President of the Royal Society. In July 1686, he is asked by the young Isaac Newton to provide the "imprimatur" (seal of approval to publish) of the Royal Society for his *Principia*. This is how Pepys' name appears on the cover page of the first edition of one of the most important scientific books ever written.[7]

---

6. *The Diary of Samuel Pepys*, ed. R. Latham and W. Matthews (Harper Collins, UC Berkeley Press, 2000), vol. IV.
7. Newton himself is President of the Royal Society by the time of the second edition of the *Principia*. Pepys' name disappears from the cover.

Figure 45: The magnificent Château Haut-Brion, the first brand-name wine of modern times (courtesy Château Haut-Brion).

Figures 46-47: The diarist Samuel Pepys, whose name is on the cover page of the first edition of Newton's Principia (© Pepys Library, Magdalene College, Cambridge)

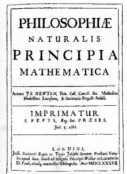

The Dutch

The Dutch are active members of the Hanseatic League since the mid 1200s. The League is an association of some 160 German, Dutch and Flemish towns which trade from the Baltic Sea to the Atlantic. The power of the league declines in the 1500s. The Dutch are then ruled by Maximilian — a Catholic Hapsburg — and Mary of Burgundy. Their son Philip marries Juana, the second daughter of the very Catholic Ferdinand and Isabella of Spain. She goes down in history as "Juana La Loca," or cazy Joanna. Their son becomes Charles I of Spain in 1516.

These unions have a direct impact on the people who live in the territories involved. Ten of the Dutch provinces are Catholic. But the seven northern ones have become Calvinist after 1567. They resent being ruled by Catholic monarchs. In 1579, they band together, form the Union of Utrecht, and turn against Spain and the Inquisition by declaring themselves independent. These "United Provinces" are today's Netherlands. They achieve independence at the treaty of Westphalia, in 1648.

With few natural resources, the Dutch turn to trade. They are very good and aggressive at it. In 1615-1616, a fleet of six Dutch warships raid Spanish colonies in America, attacking and sinking any Spanish or Portuguese ship along the way. The Dutch fat ships, known as "flyboats," hold twice as much cargo as English ships, their closest competitors. Within a century, the Dutch colonies stretch from North America — where they establish New Amsterdam, today's New York — and, by the way of Africa including the Cape, India and Ceylon, all the way to New Zealand. In Europe, they dominate the wine trade. They also establish the first wineries in South Africa.

However, in the 1600s, most wines still survive one year at best. They are light and fragile, with low alcohol and low tannin. The constant shaking and the temperature fluctuations during transport by ship often cause the wine to go bad. Sweet and fortified wines are more resilient and fetch higher prices. The Dutch encourage any innovation which helps wines survive longer.

One of them is *fortification*, which consists in adding grape alcohol to the wine. If done before the end of the fermentation, the added alcohol kills the yeast, and the residual sugar makes the wine sweet as well. The Dutch promote the *distillation* of some wines to produce the alcohol needed for fortification. The region of Armagnac already produces distilled wine since the 14th century. While the English forbid the shipping of wines on the River Garonne, except for Bordeaux wines, the shipping of brandy is allowed. The Dutch take advantage of that and purchase most of the production of Armagnac. In order to be able to provide a steady volume of distilled wines despite annual production fluctuations, the Armagnac is kept in oak barrels. The producers discover how much the quality of their product is enhanced by aging in wood.

Under Dutch influence, wine is first distilled in the region of Cognac in 1624. The Dutch also trade wines from Jerez, the region of Southern Spain where Sherry is produced. They encourage distillation and fortification there as well. The increased availability of distilled wine from these and other regions also results in the manufacture of a range of liqueurs — mixtures of distilled wine with herbs and/or fruits. Where viticulture is not successful, people distill various grains and produce vodka, whiskey, and gin.

The Dutch also encourage the fermentation of over-matured grapes — the so-called *vins pourris* ("rotten wines"). Late-harvest and over-matured grapes contain less acid and more sugar. The resulting wine has more alcohol and is often sweet. The best such wines come from the Sauternes region of Bordeaux.

The Dutch also blend light, dry, and pale wines — most of the Bordeaux wines are of that type at the time — with stronger, albeit less distinguished, "black wines" from northern Spain, Portugal or the French region of Cahors. These dark wines result from long macerations. They are more powerful and tannic.

In the 1650s the Dutch provide the technique and expertise for draining the marshes of Médoc, the so-called "*palus*" in Bordeaux. The entire region is soon covered with vineyards, destined to produce spectacular wines: Lafite, Latour, Margaux, and others are born at that time. In contrast to the light "clarets" typical of the region since medieval times, the new vineyards produce long-macerated darker, stronger wines. In the early 1700s these wines sell for 60 British pounds per tun, while the common clarets go for as little as 8 pounds.

Finally, the Dutch introduce the systematic use of *sulphur* to stabilize the wine: candles dipped in sulphur are burned inside barrels before they are filled with wine. In French, these candles are called *allumettes hollandaise* ("Dutch matches") or *mèches soufrées* ("sulphur wicks"). The sulphur kills the bacteria and yeast in the barrel. Thus, the process prevents secondary fermentation from taking place, slows down the vinegar bacteria, and prevents molds from developing.

The success of the Dutch infuriates the French and especially the English, whose trading power is seriously threatened. In the late 1670s, Europe's total merchant fleet consists of maybe 20,000 ships, of which about 15,000 are Dutch, 3,000 English, and about 500 French. In the 1660s, Jean-Baptiste Colbert, Finance Minister of Louis XIV, orders the planting of oak forests in the regions of Limousin and Tronçais to provide quality wood for a future French navy. These forests now provide the oak for wine barrels exported all over the world.

The Dutch supremacy as a naval trade power leads to protectionist legislations in Europe. Oliver Cromwell's Navigation Ordinance forbids the Dutch from shipping between English and foreign ports. Skirmishes follow, such as the "Four Days War" in 1667, when the Dutch destroy 25 English ships at the mouth of the Thames. In 1652, Cromwell declares war against the Netherlands and seizes 1,500 ships. In 1709, the English and French refuse to issue passports to the Dutch in Bordeaux, cutting them from the most profitable wine market. The Dutch continue as traders but their dominance ends.

Champagne, without the bubble

Following the onset of the Little Ice Age in the early 1300s, most vineyards in England and northern Europe are abandoned. Champagne[8] becomes the northernmost major wine region in Europe. The growing season is short, which means a high acid/sugar ratio in the fruit. Even under ideal temperature conditions during the fermentation, the alcoholic concentration is low. But the conditions are rarely ideal. The fermentation is almost never finished by the time

---

8. N. Faith, *The Story of Champagne* (Hamish-Hamilton, London, 1988).

winter arrives and the yeast goes dormant. In the spring, temperatures rise and the fermentation starts again. The result is a wine that is bubbly because of carbon dioxide and cloudy because of fermentation byproducts. Bubbles and cloudiness are regarded as signs of low quality. Ways to improve the quality and image of the wines from Champagne are sought, and the first breakthroughs are the result of the systematic work and persistence of a Benedictine monk, Pierre Dom Pérignon (1635-1715).

 In 1668, Dom Pérignon becomes procurator (administrator — that is treasurer and cellarmaster) at the Abbey of Hautvillers. He holds that position until his death in 1715. He does not drink alcohol himself, and lives on fruits and dairy products. However, he is a perfectionist dedicated to high-quality wines.

Figures 48-49: Pierre Dom Pérignon (1639-1715) and a label of the famous 1959 Cuvée Dom Pérignon champagne, a James Bond favorite.

Contrary to widespread belief, Dom Pérignon does not invent the bubbly Champagne we know today. Instead, he succeeds at producing high-quality *still* white wines in the Champagne region. His wines remain still and do not turn cloudy. He also discovers how to make white wines with black grapes.[9] He iden-

---

9. The juice of almost all grapes is colorless. The color pigments, in the skins, dissolve in the alcohol produced by the ongoing fermentation. The trick is to press the grapes and remove the skins very quickly. This is difficult to do with the technology available at the time. The result is a slightly colored wine, called *vin gris* ("grey wine").

tifies the best vineyards and systematically tests the properties of blended wines from different cultivars, including black and white grapes.[10] Later in his life, he does attempt to control the bubble in sparkling wines. He experiments with glass bottles and pioneers the use of Spanish corks in the region. However, at the time, the nature of fermentation and the critical role of sugar in the process are not understood.

Despite his brilliant work and innovations, Dom Pérignon is not interested in sales or advertising. It is Louis XIV who makes Champagne fashionable when, in 1695, he follows his doctor's advice to drink Dom Pérignon's light, white, still Champagne wines rather than rich red Burgundies.

Glass bottles

The production of thick and sturdy wine bottles is a breakthrough in the history of wine. From Neolithic times to the fall of Rome — that is for over 6,000 years — a single material is used to ferment, store, and transport wine: clay — jars, amphorae, dolia, and the like. Throughout the Middle Ages and up to the Industrial Revolution, only wood is used — casks and barrels. But in the 1600s, two materials are available: wood and glass. The maceration and fermentation can be done in wooden barrels — with the exception of champagnes which undergo a secondary fermentation in bottles, and then the wine can mature and age in glass bottles. The bottles, supplied by English merchants, are first used for Champagnes and Ports.

Bottles are of particular importance in the development of voluntarily sparkling wines.[11] The glass bottles available at the time, manufactured in Venice, Italy, are impractical for keeping wine because they are thin and fragile. Sir Kenelm Digby (1603-1665), a founding member of the Royal Society and owner of a glassworks, is credited with the invention of the first sturdy, dark-colored, onion-shaped glass bottle. The first factory-made bottles become available in England in the 1630s. The glass contains many impurities. They come from the source material (silica and a material rich in sodium or other simple metal) and from the fuel in the furnace, usually coal.

In England, the Industrial Revolution is beginning, and the demand for machinery — and therefore iron — is huge. Workable wrought-iron can only be obtained using charcoal furnaces. These furnaces are built in or near forests for obvious reasons: A single blast furnace producing 15 tons of iron a week requires an acre of forest a day for fuel. The other source of fuel, coal, contains too many impurities for the production of quality iron. The coking process[12] transforms

---

10. Today, most Champagnes are blends of wines from the white Chardonnay and the black Pinot Noir cultivars.
11. The gas pressure in a bottle of modern Champagne is of the order of 6 atmospheres.
12. Basically, it consists in heating coal in the absence of air to drive off the volatile compounds.

coal into much cleaner coke. But it still contains too much sulphur for making wrought iron. Sulphur renders red-hot iron brittle. In 1709, Abraham Darby I first smelts iron ore with coke on a commercial basis, but the first coke furnaces[13] practical for the production of wrought iron are developed much later, in 1750, by his son Abraham Darby II.

The earliest bottles have an irregular neck and the corks are tapered and inserted only part-way into the bottle. The corks can adjust to the shape of the neck and are easy to remove. The first corkscrews, originally called "bottle-screws," appear in the 1630s, at the same time bottles are manufactured. Comparable devices are already in use to remove unspent bullets from muskets.

Figure 50: Mouth-blown wine bottle from the mid-1700s (photo: Darrel Thomas)

In the 1700s, the shape of bottles changes from bubble or onion, which are designed to stay upright, to cylindrical. These bottles often have a "pun," the indentation at the bottom, which adds to their strength. The cylindrical shape allows the bottle to lie on its side. In this position, the cork remains wet inside the bottle and does not dry and shrink.[14] This isolates the wine from the air, allowing it to age, which often improves the wine substantially.

The birth of Ports

The English purchase and ship the powerful but not very distinguished wines from the dry and hot Upper Douro valley of Portugal since the 1400s. In order to improve these wines, they import French oak barrels to replace the goatskins in which the local wines are traditionally kept. Following the Dutch methods to stabilize the wine for shipping, the merchants add some brandy to the wine. In the 1600s, in order to prevent erosion and help retain moisture in the vineyards, the English also

---

13. J. Marsh (History of Science and Technology Group, University of Manchester), private communication.

begin the construction of extensive terraces, each holding two to five rows of vines.[15] Starting in the late 1600s, they import glass bottles to the region. However, glass bottles are an expensive rarity. The first port from an unblended vintage year[16] is recorded in 1734.

Figure 51: Terraces in the Upper Douro valley (courtesy: Niepoort VINHOS S.A., photo Pedro Lobo)

The story most often repeated is that in 1678, an English merchant reports that the Abbot of the monastery at Lamego, south of Régua in Baixo Corgo — the Westernmost part of the Upper Douro — adds brandy to his wine *before* the end of the fermentation. If enough brandy is added, the yeast dies and the fermentation stops. The result is a strong wine which contains residual sugar.[17] Port is born and quickly becomes very popular. Soon after, a number of English and Dutch wine merchants move their headquarters near the mouth of the Douro River, in Vila Nova de Gaia, across the Douro River from Porto:[18] Kopke (1638), Warre's (1670), Croft's (1678), Quarles Harris (1680), Taylor's (1692), Morgan (1715), Offley (1737), and many others.

---

14. Note that in ancient times clay jars and amphorae are also kept lying on their sides to keep the clay stoppers wet and preventing them from shrinking. The earliest known example of such storage, at the Godin Tepe site in the Zagros mountains of Iran, dates back to 3500 BCE.

15. Modern terraces, built with the help of dynamite and bulldozers, are wider.

16. The earliest known vintage-dated bottle dates back to 1775.

17. S. Chantal dos Santos, in *The Great Book of Wine*, ed. J. Jobe (Galahad, 1982).

18. N. Mathieson, *Port* (Chartwell Books, Edison NJ, 1999).

Figure 52: Vila Nova de Gaia, seen from the Dom Luis Bridge which links it to the city of Porto (photo SKE).

The first noble-rot wines

The beneficial role of the "noble rot" is accidentally discovered in the 1600s. The noble rot is a fungus, *Botrytis Cinerea*, which feeds on the skin of mature grapes. It makes the skins thinner, thus allowing the water to evaporate. This concentrates the sugar without affecting much the total acid content. When ready to be picked, the grains look rotten, but the juice is incredibly sweet.

Figure 53: A cluster of Sémillon grapes (a white cultivar), at an advanced stage of development of Botrytis Cinerea (photo: Jean-Luc Barde, courtesy Philippe Baly, Château Coutet).

The very first wines made from grapes attacked by the noble rot were almost certainly made in the early 1600s in Eastern Europe, probably in Tokaji (north-eastern Hungary). However, the precise period when the same tradition started in Cotnari (north-eastern Romania) is not known. The first noble-rot wines of Sauternes (south-west of France) were made in the late 1600s or early 1700s.

The accidental discovery of the benefits of noble rot in Tokaji occurs as follows. Fearing a Turkish attack, the people of Tokaj — the city, some 120 miles north-east of Budapest — flee or remain within city walls in order to avoid being captured while working in the vineyards, and then sold as slaves. The vintage is delayed and rot develops on the grapes. The winemaker, a priest called Szepsi Laczkó, decides to harvest and make wine anyway. Laczkó is lucky: the rot is *Botrytis Cinerea* and the wine is incredibly sweet and luscious. From that date on, a part of the vineyards is always allowed to rot before being harvested.

Hungary enacts its first Wine Laws under Turkish rule, in 1641. They regulate districts and the proper way to care for vineyards. The yield is low — at most, 650 gallons per acre — and the process is not without risk. If the same fungus develops before the grapes are mature (*gray rot*), the crop is ruined. In the 1660s the role of the noble rot in the production of luscious, sweet wines is recognized in Hungary for the first time, and laws for making the *Tokaji Aszú* are formulated. "Aszú" refers to the fungus as well as to the pile of rotting grapes.

But it is not enough to produce a great wine: one must also spread the word. This happens by chance, and involves again King Louis XIV of France. In 1686 the Hapsburgs expel the Turks from Buda. Now Hungary has a Catholic ruler. Ferenc Rákóczi II (1676-1735), a Protestant, leads a Hungarian revolt against the Hapsburgs (the "Kuruc rising"). He tries unsuccessfully to secure an alliance with the French against the Hapsburg. As a goodwill gesture, he gives a large amount of Tokaji Aszú to Louis XIV. The wine quickly gains a formidable reputation. In 1866, the French wine author Jullien[19] describes it in the most flattering terms: "the most esteemed of the wine of Tokay, considered with reason to be the best dessert wine [he writes "vin de liqueur"] in the world." He goes on to mention a list of competitors: "The wine of Tokay has numerous rivals: ... the cooked wines from Southern France [he is probably referring to the Vins Doux Naturels], the Italian vino santo, the cotnar from Moldavia, ... the jenorodi from Greece, the wine from Piatra [also in Romania]." He then comments that in his opinion the Tokay is superior to all these wines. It is surprising that Jullien does not include any wine from Sauternes in his comparison, especially Château d'Yquem. He also fails to include the South African Constantia. Further, his list includes noble-rot wines such as the Cotnari as well as wines obtained with very different techniques such as the Vinsanto. As for Rákóczi, he becomes Prince of

---

19. A. Jullien, *Topographie de tous les vignobles connus* (Slatkine, Genève, 1985, reprint of the 1866 Paris edition), pages 360-362.

Transylvania in 1704, loses battles against the Austrians, and lives out his life in Constantinople.

THE 1700S: REVOLUTIONS

Background

In the 1700s, European politics is quite complicated, but this affects only marginally the history of wine. For most of this century, Frederick the Great rules over Prussia and Catherine the Great over Russia. In France, Louis XIV dies in 1715, leaving the country ruined. His successors Louis XV and Louis XVI are incompetent leaders. Spain is weak and Italy is divided. England has political difficulties all over its empire. In the 1700s, boundaries change and strategic marriages are arranged, leading to wars about who should rule a given nation. The Seven Years War (1756-1763) involves all of Europe.

The power struggles leave the population in misery. This is compounded by some of the worst winters in memory. Crops are ruined, famine and disease are common. During the winter of 1708-9, all the rivers down to the south of France freeze solid and many vines die. The vineyards in Bordeaux have to be replanted. The price of wine increases sharply as the production drops. The terrible winters of 1765, 1767, 1783 and 1788 kill many trees and vines. This brings starvation to the countryside and bread riots to Paris. Many vineyards in the North of France are abandoned. The fall of the Bastille Prison in 1789 marks the beginning of the French Revolution. People are fed up with kings and emperors jockeying for power while they starve to death. Louis XVI is decapitated in 1793. The Terror follows. Order is restored by Napoleon in 1799.

As for wines, the 1700s bring very important technological innovations: today's Champagne is born, the Châteaux of Bordeaux emerge, bottles and corks become commonplace. The end of monastic viticulture in Burgundy and Champagne starts with the French Revolution. Most of the vineyards, planted by Benedictine and Cistercian monks beginning in the late 11th century, are confiscated and sold to the highest bidder. A middle-class emerges. An increasing number of vineyards are purchased by wealthy merchants. In the 1720s, *négociants* (wine merchants) open shop in Beaune. The first Champagne house, Nicolas Ruinard in Epernay, is established in 1743.

Romanée-Conti

There is one vineyard particularly close to my heart: *Romanée-Conti*. Today, it is the most prestigious Pinot Noir in the world. In an average year, the vineyard produces a mere 6,000 bottles. Its tiny 4.4 acres are within sight of the Church at Vosne-Romanée. A Pinot Noir vine from it grows in my backyard, in

Lubbock. The history of the Romanée-Conti illustrates the fate of many Burgundy vineyards.

Figure 54: The Romanée-Conti vineyard (photo: SKE).

This vineyard is first mentioned in 1512 as *Le Clos des Cinq Journaux*,[20] property of the monks of St-Vivant. Sold many times over the years, it becomes the property of the Croonenbourg family in 1651 and is renamed *Romanée* (the adjacent *La Romanée* is distinct). In 1760, Romanée is sold to Louis François de Bourbon, Prince of Conti. After the Revolution all the vineyards in Burgundy are dispossessed and sold. *Romanée* is confiscated in 1794 by the Revolutionary Republic, renamed *Romanée-Conti* in the hope that the "Conti" name will help it fetch a higher price. It is auctioned off in July of the same year. Its wine already enjoys a fantastic reputation at the time. By the turn of the 19th century, the vineyard belongs to the Oratoire of Dijon and is named *Au-dessus de la Romanée*. It is now *Romanée-Conti* again.[21] Following the French Revolution and the Terror, the market for expensive wines plummets as most of the wealthy nobility has either fled or been killed. The prices of quality wines drop to the same level as those of bad wines. Quality wines are hard to find for over a decade.[22]

---

20. The adjacent Romanée St. Vivant vineyard is also known as Les Quatres Journaux.

21. An attempt at producing a Californian Romanée-Conti, "Clos De La Tech," involves low yields and fermentation with stems.

22. R. Dion, *Histoire de la vigne et du vin en France des Origines au 19è Siècle* (Flammarion, Paris, 1959).

Intentionally sparkling Champagne

Following the innovations of Dom Pérignon and the availability of higher-quality bottles, intentionally sparkling white wines begin to be produced in Champagne.[23] The transition from barrels to bottles takes time. Champagne is primarily sold in barrels until the mid-18th century, despite the fact that wine survives much longer in bottles than in barrels. One reason is that bottles and corks are expensive and not always of good quality. Another reason is that wine sold in bottles is much more expensive that in barrels, and therefore aimed at the wealthy customer, who demands quality. Bottled wine must be racked[24] and fined[25] several times in order to achieve the desired clarity. This means a lot of additional work. Further, there is a high risk of breakage. Indeed, in order to produce a pleasantly sparkling wine, one must bottle it with just the right amount of added sugar. The sugar triggers a secondary fermentation in the bottle, which results in dissolved CO_2 gas, the desired bubble. But how much sugar is "right" is anybody's guess. The precise amount needed depends on how much residual sugar is still in the wine when it is bottled, something neither understood nor measurable at the time. Too little sugar results in a flat wine. Too much of it causes the CO_2 pressure to build up and the bottle to explode. The explosion of a bottle is a very loud and powerful event, which can trigger the explosion of nearby bottles, resulting in a chain reaction. In a typical year, as many as one-third to one-half of the bottles explode in the spring! Even when the process is successful, the secondary fermentation in the bottle leaves unsightly[26] lees which render the wine cloudy. Producing "modern" champagne is a lot of work.

The standard champagne bottle, with a cork tied to its necks, is introduced in 1735, but the use of bottles really picks up after 1750. In 1780, De Maizière discovers that blending wines from different Champagne regions allows a better control of the gas pressure and reduces the breakage. As a result, over a quarter-million bottles of champagne are produced in 1788.

The target customer for the bubbly Champagne is the upper-class woman. It is said that the Champagne "coupes," the short and wide glasses, are modeled after the breasts of Marie Antoinette,[27] wife of Louis XVI. This story may be the reason why Champagne coupes are traditionally used at weddings. The elon-

---

23. N. Faith, *The Story of Champagne* (Hamish-Hamilton, London, 1988).
24. Racking is the transfer of wine from one barrel to another, leaving as much lees behind as possible.
25. Fining involves pouring a "glue" (such as egg whites) into a barrel. It traps unwanted impurities as it drops to the bottom.
26. Lees are the deposit at the bottom of barrels or bottles: dead yeast, minerals, remaining solid bits of grape skins, etc.
27. She is guillotined in 1794.

gated Champagne "flûte" is much more appropriate for enjoying this wine, as its shape allows bubbles to survive longer.

[champagne is] the only wine that leaves a woman beautiful after drinking it.
—Madame de Pompadour (1721-1764), mistress of Louis XV

Grands Crus in Bordeaux

❧The first records of a specific property in Bordeaux appear in the 17th century. Before then, most Bordeaux wines were simply labeled "claret," a word still used today for Bordeaux wine in England. A few Bordeaux wines are named after the main town in the area of production. Six regions within Bordeaux are recognized: Graves, Palu, Entre-deux-Mers, Langon, Barsac, and Preignac. A few brand-name wines are known, most importantly Haut-Brion (Samuel Pepys' "Ho Bryan"), Lafite, Margaux ("Margo").

Haut-Brion is the property of the Pontac family, wealthy landowners involved in local politics. In winemaking, they follow the Dutch emphasis on "black wines." These are obtained from long macerations which give more color and tannin. These wines have a much longer life than the traditional light-colored clarets. Producing deep-color wines becomes a trend in the region.

The idea of creating "Grand Cru" deep red wines aimed at wealthy customers emerges at Château Margaux in the 1730s. The concept catches on because there is a demand for such wines. Neighboring winemakers fight for prestige, name recognition and markets. Spectacular buildings are constructed and the concept of "château" appears. This competition has been labeled the "Second Hundred Years War" or the "War of the Châteaux." It culminates with the classification of 1855 (see below).

In addition to Grand Cru red wines, high-quality sweet wines are also becoming available. The most important of them is Château d'Yquem, which produces noble-rot wines. The Yquem property dates back to 1593, when Jacques de Sauvage acquires "*la maison appellée Yquem*," then property of the Crown of France. "Lur-Saluce" appears on the label after 1785, following the marriage of Françoise Joséphine de Sauvage to Louis Amédée de Lur-Saluce, the godson of Louis XV. Yquem is famous for late-harvest wines since its earliest days. The Dutch did encourage the production of sweet wines by paying a premium for them. However, allowing the grains to rot goes beyond a standard late harvest. When a noble rot harvest first occurs in Sauternes is not sure. The story is that Lur-Saluce leaves for military duty and returns a month late for harvest. His workers wait for instructions while the noble rot develops.

Even though noble rot wines are produced at Yquem in the early 1700s, the origin of the luscious taste is not advertised for fear of turning off a key customer: the Church. The sweet wine of Yquem is often the holy wine of the Sacrament, and the use of rotten grapes to produce this wine might have been deemed inappropriate. By the 1740s, the grape pickers receive detailed instructions on how to select individual, perfectly "roasted" grains and are ordered to keep their mouth shut.[28]

The reputation of the fabulous Château d'Yquem is well established by the time Thomas Jefferson, American ambassador to France, wine lover and future President of the United States, visits the region in the 1780s. He is so impressed by Château d'Yquem that he orders 30 bottles for George Washington's presidential cellar – and ten dozen cases for himself at the embassy.

Ports

The fortification of wines from the Upper Douro valley with brandy is routinely done since the 1500s. Since 1678, it is also known that if enough brandy is added to the wine before the end of the fermentation, the added alcohol kills the yeast and stops the fermentation, thus leaving some of the natural sugar in the wine. This fortification process is routinely done since then. In 1703, a commercial treaty between Portugal and England, the Methuen Treaty, is signed in Lisbon. It establishes that English textiles are accepted in Portugal while Portuguese wines exported to England are taxed at only two-third the rate applied to French wines. Soon, over half the wine arriving in England is from Portugal. The production of ports immediately increases and, with it, fraud. Cheap alcohol replaces quality brandy for fortification, elderberry juice is added for color and dried pimento for power. The drop in quality is followed by a drop in demand, then in prices, which collapse around 1750. The reputation of Port wines plummets.

The massive Lisbon earthquake, estimated at 8.5 on the Richter scale,[29] and tsunami of November 1, 1755 kills some 40,000 people out of a population of about 275,000. The Prime Minister of King Joseph I, Sebastião de Carvalho, the authoritarian Marquis of Pombal (1699-1782), takes control of the country. He supervises the reconstruction of Lisbon, curbs the power of the Inquisition, expels the Jesuits, ends slavery in Portugal, and reforms the study of Sciences.

Pombal also imposes a wine monopoly in Porto, sets strict regulations about the production and export of Ports, and limits the areas where port is allowed to be produced. This results in a near revolution in Porto, where the English and Dutch merchants are used to act as they please. Pombal crushes the rebellion.

Pombal's dictatorial manners earn him a lot of enemies. King Joseph dies in 1777. His daughter becomes the new monarch, Maria I. She pardons all the political prisoners. Pombal is tried and banished. His regulations, the first large-scale government control over wine and vineyards, are abandoned and the

---

28. *Rules of Cultivation of Château Filhot*, 1740 (Filhot was a property of Château d'Yquem). See J. Benson and A. Mackenzie, *Sauternes* (Sotheby's, London, 1990).
29. Science **302**, 1295 (2003); Bull. Seismol. Soc. Am. **93**, 2056 (2003).

quality of Port wines drops again. Serious government regulations are reinstated in 1907 by Joao Franco, Prime Minister of King Carlos I.

Figure 55: Sebastião de Carvalho, Marquis of Pombal (wood engraving by Severini, done in 1882 as part of the 100-year commemoration of Pombal's death. (Courtesy João Campos Gil)

THE 1800S TO WORLD WAR II: INNOVATIONS AND DISASTERS

Overview

The dawn of the 19th century coincides with the rise of Napoleon. Fifteen years of wars consume Europe, from Lisbon to Moscow. Following his defeat at Waterloo in 1815, the Emperor is sent into his final exile to the island of St. Helena. Napoleon's main wine legacy is the abolishment of the medieval "Salic code" by which a father's entire inheritance goes to his eldest son. He replaces it with the "Law of Equal Inheritance" by which all property must be equally divided among the male children. This results in the fragmentation of many vineyards, the consequences of which are particularly obvious in Burgundy. After a few generations, any estate large enough to sustain a family becomes a patchwork of tiny properties, each one too small to sustain a business. This leads to extreme situations such as Clos de Vougeot, a 124-acre vineyard with over 80 owners.[30]

From 1815 to 1848, revolutionary movements pop up across Europe. In France, the monarchy returns, but Louis XVIII is a weak king. His brother Charles X succeeds him in 1824 and attempts to restore an absolute monarchy. Mobs send him fleeing to England in 1830. He is replaced by Louis Philippe. The year 1848 sees revolutions throughout Europe. Karl Marx publishes the *Com-*

---

30. A. Hanson, *Burgundy* (Faber and Faber, London, 1982).

munist Manifesto. The 1848 French revolution marks the beginning of the Second Republic, with Louis-Napoleon as president. He establishes the Second Empire in 1852, and names himself Emperor Napoleon III. The Third Republic replaces the Second Empire in 1870.

In 1914 Archduke Ferdinand, heir to the Austro-Hungarian throne, is assassinated in Sarajevo by a Bosnian Serb nationalist. This touches off the events that lead to World War I, the bloody war that has no real reason to begin, ends by sheer exhaustion, and firmly plants the seeds of World War II. Between the two World Wars, maps and atlases in German schools describe the regions of Alsace and Lorraine as "temporarily under French control."

The general poverty and despair that follow World War I result in widespread alcoholism. Many governments push some form of prohibition. The Finnish Diet forbids the import of alcoholic beverages in 1910. Several northern European countries heavily tax alcohol and restrict its sale to state-run stores. The United States amends its Constitution.

In 1922, Benito Mussolini seizes power in Italy. The Great Depression begins after the stock market crash in 1929. Constantinople becomes Istanbul on March 28, 1930. In Spain, the 1931 republican victory in municipal elections results in King Alfons XIII being deposed and the Second Republic established. Five years of chaos follow and culminate in Francisco Franco's (1898-1975) *Manifesto* and the Spanish Civil War (1933-1936). Starting in 1933, Japan and Germany violate the spirit of the League of Nations by rebuilding their military and by aggression. World War II follows.

❧The first half of the 19th century is uneventful for wines. After the very cold 1805-1820 years, wines benefit from better weather and trade. A canal system is built in Burgundy and the new Paris-Dijon railway, finished in 1851, facilitates commerce.[31] In 1855, Dr. Jules Lavalle publishes the first unofficial ranking of Burgundy's vineyards. The same year, in Bordeaux, Napoleon III orders a classification of the best Médoc wines. The scientific studies of Louis Pasteur (and others) lead to the understanding of fermentation and the roles of sugar and oxygen. In 1866, André Jullien published the final edition of his *Topographie*,[32] which describes all the known vineyards in the world at the time. Jullien also ranks the wines of every region on a scale of one (top rank) to four. This snapshot of the global situation is very timely indeed, as the world of wine and viticulture is about to be completely transformed by Phylloxera. Michael Owens perfects a machine capable of mass-producing glass bottles.

❧ Just as the future of wine looks bright, a series of calamities nearly destroy it. A fungus new to Europe, *powdery mildew*, arrives from America and destroys

---

31. The Paris-Bordeaux railway is operational in 1853. Most of France is connected to the national railway system in 1875.
32. A. Jullien, *Topographie de tous les vignobles connus* (Slatkine, Genève, 1985, reprint of the 1866 Paris edition.

many vineyards. Then, the tiny louse *phylloxera vastatrix*, also from North America, devastates *v. vinifera* all around the world. Finally, *downy mildew* arrives. Just as the situation begins to improve, World War I brings devastation and poverty, and the Russian Revolution shuts off the profitable Russian market. Then come Prohibition, the Great Depression, and World War II.

Science and technology

Scientific and technological advances abound in the 19th century. In 1800, Alessandro Volta discovers the electric battery, thus making electricity practical. In 1831, Michael Faraday invents the dynamo. In 1876, the first telegraph appears. The Industrial Revolution is in full swing. People migrate from the countryside to the cities.

⚘At the very beginning of the 1800s, the French chemist Jean-Autoine Chaptal (1756-1832) recommends adding some sugar to the must before or during fermentation, as this increases the alcohol content of the wine without affecting its taste. The procedure, called "chaptalization," is legal in France and used in all but the warmest vintage years. Chaptal also discusses techniques for proper fermentation, raking, and preservation of wines.

⚘Louis Pasteur (1822-1895) studies fermentation and oxidation. In 1857, he discovers the basic chemical reaction in fermentation.[33] The sugar in the must is food for yeast, which breaks it into alcohol (ethanol) and carbon dioxide gas: $C_6H_{12}O_6 \rightarrow 2C_2H_5OH + 2CO_2$. In 1895, Emile Manceau at the Moët champagne house and, independently in 1897, Eduard and Hans Buchner, discover that yeast only produces the enzymes which actually perform the fermentation. Pasteur spends years studying wine. He identifies several of its key components and explains how oxygen transforms wine into vinegar, but also that it plays an essential role in the aging of wine.

⚘ Bottle technology improves. The early wine bottles of the mid-1600s are designed to stand upright. Their shape evolves over time to allow *binning*, which is the storing of wine in bottles lying on their side. In this position, the wine keeps the cork moist inside the bottle, thus preventing it from shrinking. The wine can age, protected from contact with the outside air. However, the capacity of the blown or molded bottles is irregular. English laws dating back to 1636 forbid the sale of wine in bottles. Wine is sold by measure. Many people own bottles marked with a seal, such as their initials or heraldic sign. In 1821,

---

33. The French chemist and tax collector Antoine-Laurent Lavoisier (1743-1794) first formulates the idea that chemical reactions are transformations of pre-existing elements by rearrangement. He believes that fermentation involves the rearrangement of the elements making up sugar in order to create alcohol, carbon dioxide and other byproducts. Pasteur quantifies this statement and recognizes that biological processes occur as well. Lavoisier is guillotined in 1794 during the policies of Terror that follow the French Revolution.

Ricketts of Bristol patents a machine for molding bottles of uniform shape and size, but it is not until 1860 that selling wine by the bottle becomes legal. Hand-written wine labels first appear in the early 1800s. Printed ones become common in the latter part of the century.

Figure 56: Louis Pasteur (1822-1895)

₰ The large-scale production of molded bottles becomes possible with an American invention, the "Owens machine." Michael J. Owens' (1859-1923) first fully automatic bottle-making machine is built in 1903. An improved version (1912) produces over 50,000 bottles a day, that is 35 bottles a minute. This is quite an achievement, especially since the complex machine operates at the temperature of molten glass. The last Owens machines stop operation in 1982.

Figure 57: The Ten Arm Owens Machine (photo: Lewis W. Hine, c. 1913. © Albin O. Kuhn Library, University of Maryland).

Nature-made disasters

Vitis vinifera vinifera, the species to which virtually all the wine cultivars belong, is a descendent of the wild *v.v. sylvestris*, native to the Near East and Europe. In contrast, there are a dozen distinct species of vines in North America: *v. labrusca, v. rupestris, v. riparia*, etc. *V. vinifera* cannot survive there unless grafted onto American rootstock. The reasons are North American bacteria, fungi, and insects which are deadly to the European species. Over time, the native American varieties developed resistance to the local threats, or died. The

European species, never exposed to them, is very vulnerable. In the 1800s, commercial exchanges between Europe and North American increase. This includes shipments of timber and plants. It is only a matter of time before fungi or pests new to Europe arrive from America.

‌‌*Powdery mildew*, or *oidium*, arrives in England in 1845, then in France in 1847. By 1850, it is endemic in much of Europe and the Near East. This fungus attacks all parts of the vine. Wine production takes a nosedive. By 1852, the harvest is down by about 80%, and the 1854 vintage is the smallest since the frigid 1788. Trial and error leads to the spraying with a mixture of sulphur, lime and water. This controls the fungus, but it is still a problem today, especially in wet years.

Phylloxera is first noticed in 1863 in southern Côtes du Rhône, where it probably arrived with imported American rootstock. It is a tiny root-feeding aphid, which does not do well in sandy soil but thrives elsewhere. The female is about four-hundredths of an inch in size and produces several hundred eggs, three to five times per year. It would be difficult to see her chewing on roots were it not for the mass of eggs that surrounds her.

Phylloxera crawls from vine to vine and can be carried by the wind, but its most efficient mode of transportation is man, by transporting infested plant matter or more simply on the sole of shoes or dirty tools. One after the other, almost all the vineyards in the world are hit: France in 1863, the Douro region of Portugal in 1868, Turkey in 1871, Austria in 1872, Switzerland in 1874, Italy in 1875, Australia and parts of Spain in 1877, Algeria, South Africa and New Zealand in 1885, Greece in 1898. Phylloxera spares a few islands (Crete, Cyprus, Rhodes) as well as a handful of vineyards in France and Portugal, sometimes surrounded by affected ones. It is not clear why some specific locations are immune to the pest. In Champagne for example, the Clos Chaudes Terres and Clos St. Jacques (pinot noir) are still not grafted today. There are also a few vineyards in Touraine planted with prephylloxera Romorantin vines and gamay. In Portugal the small wine region of Colares north-west of Lisbon on the Atlantic coast is not affected, and neither are a couple of vineyards at Quinta do Noval. The port they produce is labeled "Nacional" because the roots are Portuguese. In Spain, some vines in Rías Baixas (in the north-west) are also not grafted. There is no phylloxera threat in Chile,[34] but Argentina is affected.

In France, phylloxera destroys 6.2 million acres of vines from 1875 to 1889 and the production drops from 2.2 billion to 600 million gallons. The 1868 Commission identifies phylloxera as the culprit. Everything imaginable is tried to control it: spraying with various chemicals, flooding vineyards with seawater for periods of up to two months, or even planting a live toad beneath each vine.

---

34. According to S. Geneste (Los Boldos Winery), several reasons contribute to the absence of phylloxera in Chile. It is geographically protected by the Andes and the Pacific Ocean, the climate is very dry, irrigation drowns the aphid, and soil contains minerals and metals (such as copper) which affect phylloxera.

(This scientifically questionable idea originates from the thought that toad venom might kill the bug.) Even though flooding the vineyards does provide some temporary protection, it obviously does not work for the best vineyards, which are located on hillsides. No practical solution is found.

Figures 58-59: Powdery mildew on leaf and fruit (photo: Edward Hellman, Texas Tech University).

The American entomologist Charles Riley[35] suggests grafting European varieties on American rootstock. Indeed, American vines remain healthy even when growing next to affected French vines. The degree of resistance of an American vine relates to the toughness of its wood. *V. vulpania* is entirely immune, but it is nearly impossible to use for grafting. *V. aestivalis* and *v. riparia* are highly resistant, while *v. labrusca* is much less. Ultimately, *v. riparia* is selected for its good phylloxera resistance and suitability for accepting grafts.[36]

⬤The 1881 Phylloxera Congress in Bordeaux discusses chemical means of control and, reluctantly, the grafting of French vines onto American rootstock. Most French growers resist the idea of importing the inferior[37] American vines to Europe and fear that the quality of wines will be irreparably compromised. Some growers create American-*vinifera* hybrids, the so-called "French hybrids."

---

35. Charles Valentine Riley (1843-1895) is born in England and educated in France and Germany. He becomes the State entomologist of Missouri in 1869.
36. When phylloxera arrives in California in the 1870s, it is *v. rupestris*, better suited to the dry climate, that becomes the preferred source of rootstock.
37. "Inferior" refers to the quality of the wine produced by American vines. Obviously, the vines themselves are superior in terms of resistance to phylloxera.

These provide only moderate phylloxera resistance and the quality of the wine they produce is definitely lower than that of *vinifera* vines.

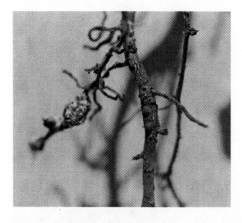

Figures 60-61: Infestation of Phylloxera Vastatrix on roots with detail enlarged (photo: Edward Hellman, Texas Tech University).

Reluctantly, the grafting of v. *vinifera* onto American rootstock begins, not just in Europe but throughout the world. This involves enormous quantities of American rootstock. In France, 6,200 acres are grafted in 1880, and 110,000 by 1885. One positive side of this situation is that replanting of all the vineyards involves quality cultivars well-suited to the local climate. The grafting is still done today, almost everywhere, as it is the only known way to grow *vinifera* in the presence of phylloxera.

In Cognac, the issue is to find phylloxera-resistant rootstock that also thrives in the chalky soil of the region. The solution comes from the small town of Denison in Texas, near the Oklahoma border, where Thomas Munson (1843-1913) is experimenting with vine rootstocks. His collaboration with the French Pierre Viala results in the identification of the best rootstock for the region of Cognac. Munson, credited with saving Cognac, receives the French Legion of Merit in 1888. The cities of Denison and Cognac are twinned since 1993.

As Europe imports thousands of tons of American rootstock to save its cultivars from phylloxera, a new problem crosses the Atlantic on the imported vines: *downy mildew*. This fungus attacks young leaves and fruits, and thrives in warm, humid summers. It first appears in 1878, and still is a problem today.

This fungus is controlled by spraying the *Bordeaux Mixture*, a blend of lime, copper, sulphur and water. Nevertheless, it is responsible for the low yields in wet years. The systematic spraying of vineyards with sulphur dates back to the Powdery and Downy mildew. Because of this, almost no wine is totally free of sulfites. The exceptions are the noble-rot wines, since these mixtures would inhibit the growth of the Noble Rot, *Botrytis Cinerea*.

Figure 62: Thomas V. Munsen (courtesy : Bureau National Interprofessionnel du Cognac)

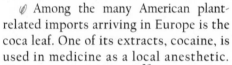

Figures 63-64: Downy mildew on leaf and fruit (photo: Edward Hellman, Texas Tech University).

📖 Among the many American plant-related imports arriving in Europe is the coca leaf. One of its extracts, cocaine, is used in medicine as a local anesthetic. There are many other uses.[38] The Corsican Angelo Mariani, a large importer and grower of coca, has an idea that turns out to be very lucrative. He soaks coca leaves in Bordeaux wine and sells the result under the name *Vin Mariani*, which he claims "Nourishes — Fortifies — Refreshes — Aids Digestion — Strengthens the System." His wine becomes immensely popular, and a large number of consumers praise it in writing. Mariani keeps the flattering comments from heads of state, religious figures, writers, artists, scientists. The list of enthusiastic supporters includes Prince Albert I of Monaco, King Alfons XIII of Spain, Shah Mozaffer-al-Dine of Persia, Tsar Nicholas II of Russia, Popes Pius X and Leo XIII, Jules Verne, H.G. Wells, Thomas Edison, and many others. His concoction not only stimulates the drinkers but also generates copycats. Of notice is the "French Wine Cola" of John Styth Pemberton (1830-1888). It contains Bordeaux wine soaked in coca leaves as well as caffeine from the cola nut. In 1885, the prohibitionists in Atlanta object to the presence of wine in the mix. Pemberton replaces it with fruit juice, citric acid and sugar. Coca-Cola is born.[39]

---

38. J. Kennedy, *Coca Exotica* (Fairleigh Dickinson University Press, Rutherford, 1985).

Champagne

In the 1800s, winemakers in Champagne fine-tune their processes, armed with the legacy of Dom Pérignon and a better control of the bubble. One of the most colorful characters in the early 1800s is the great Veuve Cliquot-Ponsardin. She marries François Cliquot in 1799, but her husband dies in 1805. She takes over his Champagne business, a decidedly male occupation at the time. Over the years, she earns a solid reputation and gains considerable respect from everybody.

Figure 65: Madame Cliquot-Ponsardin, by Léon Cogniet (courtesy: Maison Veuve Clicquot).

The first "pupitres de remuage" are invented at *Veuve Cliquot* around 1813. In these devices, the bottles are placed neck down at increasingly sharp angles on a specially-designed rack, and are gently shaken ("riddled"). A professional riddler can shake some 40,000 bottles daily! These clever devices force the lees to precipitate in the neck of the bottle, making it easier to remove them. This removal, called *disgorgement*,[40] is first proposed by André Simon. To compensate for the small loss of wine that results, the bottle if topped-off with a small amount of Cognac. This adds strength and some color to the Champagne.

In 1820 better-designed corks are produced by gluing together more than one piece of cork in the desired shape. Corking machines become available. By 1850, the corks are branded and the wire muzzles applied by machine. In order to induce the secondary fermentation in bottles needed to produce the CO_2 bubbles characteristic of Champagne, a small amount of sweet liqueur (*liqueur de tirage*) is added to the wine. Too little sugar produces flat Champagne, and too much of it results in substantial CO_2 pressure which can lead the bottles to explode. The combination of stronger bottles and more accurate estimates of the

---

39. There is no more coca leaf infusion in Coca-Cola since 1902, but a (legal) flavoring agent from the coca leaf is still used.
40. Before the disgorgement technique was perfected, the wine had to be decanted to remove the lees, a process during which the carbon dioxide pressure is substantially reduced.

amount of liqueur needed reduce the breakage to about 15% by 1837. But accidents still happen: in 1928 too much sugar is used and nearly 80% of the bottles explode, an event remembered as "*La Grande Casse*" (the great breakage). In 1895 a scientist at Moët achieves consistent onsets of secondary fermentation (*prise de mousse*) by selecting yeasts from various regions. By the late 1800s, Champagne as we know it is sold.

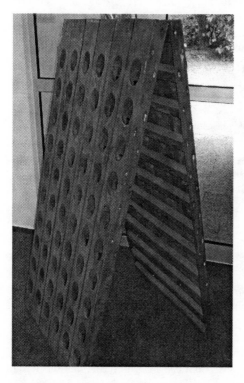

Figure 66: A "pupitre de remuage": the bottles, positioned at varying angles, are gently shaken and given 1/8 of a turn daily (photo SKE).

During the secondary fermentation and aging, the Champagne bottles are kept in deep caves. They earliest ones were carved in the chalk by the Romans! Today, there are many miles of caves under the city of Reims, and millions of bottles of champagne are kept underground.

Mercier, the owner of the Mercier Champagne House, comes up with publicity stunts that are well ahead of his time.[41] For the 1889 Universal Exposition in Paris, he builds a huge barrel, 200,000-bottle capacity, which is towed to Paris by 24 oxen. The three-week trip is a sensation, especially when an axle breaks, blocking a Paris street for days. At the 1900 Exposition, the Mercier tasting room is set in the gondola of a huge hot-air balloon. On a windy day, the cables snap, and the balloon takes off with the gondola, the bartender, and several customers. It crashes 16 days later in Austria. Mercier is fined 20 crowns for illegally importing Champagne across the border.

Because of the technological advances in the manufacture of Champagne, clever marketing, and publicity events such as those, the awareness of Champagne wines grows tremendously between 1850 and World War I. However, there are many problems. After 1855, powdery mildew dramatically reduces the yields. Winemakers import wines, and the quality of Champagne drops. The

41. N. Faith, *The Story of Champagne* (Hamish-Hamilton, London, 1988).

Franco-Prussian War of 1870 temporarily interrupts the increase in sales. The regions of Alsace and Lorraine become German at the end of the War in 1871. When phylloxera arrives in 1890, all the vineyards have to be uprooted. In Alsace, the German impose the planting of American-European hybrid cultivars and restrict the planting to flat regions which can be flooded to control phylloxera. The quality of Alsatian wines drops precipitously. In Champagne and Alsace, the 1908 vintage is poor, the grapes rot in 1909, and almost no wine is produced in 1910. Soon after, World War I begins.

The Great War devastates the region. For four years, trenches are everywhere. Long and bloody battles, such as the Marne, rage in the heart of the Champagne vineyards. Somehow, grapes are picked and wine is made. It is said that the 1914 and 1915 champagnes "have the blood of France running through them." At the end of the war, Alsace and Lorraine become French again.

Regulations aimed at protecting the brand name "Champagne" appear after World War I. The Champagne area is delimited in 1925. The law allows only the Pinot Noir, Pinot Meunier and Chardonnay cultivars to be grown. The use of the inferior Gamay is discontinued. A slow renaissance begins. In 1921, Moët produces the first cases of a new luxury brand, *Dom Pérignon*. It reaches the market in 1936. But World War II begins in 1939. France is invaded in 1940. Looted wines make their way to Germany.[42]

Classifications in Bordeaux

The earliest classification of Bordeaux wines[43] dates back to the early 1700s. It is found in the notes of Basin de Bezuns, intendant of Louis XIV. A 1770 ranking by Lawton is refined in 1787 by none other than Thomas Jefferson, recognized in the US and in France as a real wine connoisseur. Jefferson's travel notes include a ranking of the red wines from Bordeaux. His four top red wines, Châteaux Haut-Brion, Latour, Lafite, and Margaux, are also the top-classified wines in 1855. Jefferson also notes that old vines produce better wines than young ones.

In 1855, Napoleon III orders a classification of the best Bordeaux wines which he wants to show off at the Universal Exposition in Paris. The classification of 1855 is done by the *Syndicat des Courtiers en Vin de Bordeaux*. It includes the districts of Médoc, Haut-Médoc, and Sauternes. Château Haut-Brion from Graves, famous since two centuries, is also included. The ranking is based on the prices fetched by the wines over the previous hundred years or more, as given in the official records.

---

42. D. and P. Kladstrup, *Wine and War* (Broadway Books, New York, 2001).
43. R. Lebeau, *Historia* **73**, 58 (2001).

The best Médoc wines are divided into First through Fifth growths.[44] In 1855, the First growths are Châteaux Lafite-Rothschild, Latour, Margaux, and Haut-Brion. The first of the Second growths is a relative newcomer, Mouton-Rothschild. The Sauternes are divided into three classes, and the top class consists of a single name: Château d'Yquem. Wines in several other (but not all) Bordeaux regions are ranked or classified in the 1950s, using different schemes (Appendix B).

❦ The 1860s are prosperous for Bordeaux. An Anglo-French treaty signed that year reduces tariffs and facilitates exports. New markets emerged in Russia and the Americas. However, in the late 1860s, mildew and phylloxera arrive, and the production plummets. Winemakers blend the few wines they produce with Spanish and Algerian wines, and use excess amounts of fertilizers. The quality drops. Bordeaux suffers through the end of World War II, albeit much less than Champagne or Burgundy, as no major battle is fought near Bordeaux.

❦ The story of Bordeaux is incomplete without mention of the Rothschild's.[45] The founders of the dynasty are the bankers Mayer Amschel and Gütele Schnapper, in Frankfurt. They send their five sons to the strategic financial centers of the time: Amschel Jr. stays in Frankfurt, Salomon goes to Vienna, Carl to Naples, Nathan to London, and James to Paris. The latter buys Château Lafite in 1868, and dies shortly thereafter. His descendants Edmond (1845-1934) then Elie (1917-) rename it Lafite-Rothschild.

Figure 67: The spectacular Château d'Yquem (courtesy: Château d'Yquem).

In 1863, Nathan's son Nathaniel purchases the 86-acre Brane-Mouton in Bordeaux and renames it Mouton-Rothschild. Its wine is classified first of the Second growths in 1855. Mouton Rothschild's motto is:

Premier ne puis,
Second ne daigne,
Mouton suis.
(First I cannot be, Second I do not deign, I am Mouton.)

---

44. "Growth" is a translation of the French *cru*, which itself derives from *croître*, to grow. *Cru* may refer to a particular estate, to the château itself, or to the wine made from the grapes that grow there. In Burgundy, the word *climat* is used instead of *cru*.
45. N. Ferguson, *The House of Rothschild* (Penguin, 1998).

Nathaniel dies in 1870. His son James II begins the construction of the château in 1882. His widow Thérèse finishes it. Their son Henri, a doctor, shows little interest in the property. In 1922, he orders his son Philippe to care for it. There is no electricity, running water, or even decent roads. Yet, two years later, Philippe produces his first "chateau-bottled" wines. Over time, the property grows with the acquisition of Châteaux d'Armailhacq (1933) and Clerc Milon (1970).

Baron Philippe's goal is to make of Mouton-Rothschild the best and most respected Bordeaux wine. He wants to make it a wine equal in prestige to the Lafite, which belongs to his cousins, descendents of James I. The campaign begins in 1953 and lasts 20 years. This goal is finally reached on June 21, 1973, when Secretary of Agriculture Jacques Chirac signs the only change in the 1855 Classification. Château Mouton Rothschild is now classified as a First Growth. Its motto changes to:

> *Premier je suis,*
> *Second je fus,*
> *Mouton ne change*

(First I am, Second I was, Mouton does not change).

Figure 68: Baron Philippe de Rothschild in his vineyards around 1952 (courtesy: Château Mouton Rothschild)

Baron Philippe fights to impose château-bottling for all Bordeaux wines, an uphill battle against wine dealers. At the age of 24, he manages to convince the owners of the prestigious Châteaux Lafite, Haut-Brion, Margaux, Latour, and Yquem to stop selling their wine in bulk and instead bottle the wine themselves. All the châteaux in Bordeaux eventually have to adopt château-bottling.

The label on the first château-bottled Mouton is illustrated by Jean Carlu. This marks the beginning of the "artist series" of Mouton labels, which now includes Chagall, Picasso, Dali, Cocteau, Warhol, and many others. The few vintage years with no artist-decorated label are 1945 (it has the "V" of victory), 1953 (the centennial year), and 1977 (it marks the visit of Queen Elizabeth). In 1970, Baron Philippe suggests the possibility of a joint venture to Napa Valley's

Robert Mondavi. The result is Opus One, and the first vintage year is 1979. It is the first of a number of European-Californian joint ventures.

Figure 69: Some of the artist-decorated Mouton-Rothschild labels (from left to right): Hans Erni (1987), Keith Haring (1988), Georg Baselitz (1989), and Francis Bacon (1990) (photo SKE).

Wine regulations in France emerge from necessity. Following mildew and phylloxera, the volume of wine produced drops substantially in all wine-growing regions. In France, the winegrowers form cooperatives in order to help each other and maintain minimum prices, which reach ridiculously low levels after World War I. But the cooperatives are often too small to control market forces. This encourages the blending of lesser wines to brand-name wines in order to increase the volume. This further decreases the quality of the product, adding downward pressure on already low prices. A majority of the wines found on the market are seriously adulterated. The situation seems hopeless.

In 1905, 1919, and 1927, the French government enacts laws with the intent to stop the fraud, such as the blending of French with Algerian or Spanish wines, and impose geographical delimitations. These laws are not strictly enforced, as the government has more pressing priorities.

In modern times, governmental regulations related to wine date back to the mid-1400s when Philippe the Good, Duke of Burgundy, dictates where the Pinot Noir and Gamay cultivars can and cannot be planted. The Hungarian Wine Laws of 1641 come next. In 1716, Grand Duke Cosimo III of Tuscany delimits the Chianti Classico region. The first delimitation of port wines by the Marquis of Pombal follows the 1755 Lisbon earthquake. Thus, the idea of quality control through government regulations is not new. But the regulations are neither widespread nor enforced. In the early 1900s, such control is badly needed.

In the mid-1930s, a *négociant* (wine dealer) in Burgundy, Maurice Drouhin, decides to go against the grain and focus on quality. He purchases almost two-thirds of the production from the famous Domaine de la Romanée-Conti, and refuses to manipulate the wine or sell it at bargain-based price. His idea takes hold and a number of *négociants* follow his lead. They developed the concept of *Appellation d'Origine Contrôlée*: a guarantee of origin, and therefore quality, for wines.

The French law of 1935 creates the INAO (*Institut National des Appellations Contrôlées*) which codifies the *Appellation d'Origine Contrôlée* (AOC or AO) system. The law has been revised and expanded several times since then. The law dictates which regions have the AOC label and which cultivars are allowed. The wines produced in the AOC regions must obey strict rules governing the use of fertilizers, the maximum number of vines per acre, the type and severity of the pruning, the maximum yield, the minimum alcohol content, and other aspects of winemaking. The law spells out which cultivars are allowed in each region. You cannot grow Chardonnay in Bordeaux or Cabernet Sauvignon in Burgundy for example. The wines have to be labeled using geographical names, not cultivars (the exception is Alsace). The AOC system is designed to force winemakers to produce high quality by imposing a strict maximum yield. Prices finally go up. The AOC laws are strictly enforced today. For example, any production in excess of the allowed yield cannot be sold, even for distillation: it must be given or thrown away.

In most AOC regions, wines are labeled by geographical name: The more specific the area, the higher the quality of the wine and the stricter the rules. In Burgundy for example, a wine named after a region ("Burgundy") is of a lower rank than a wine labeled by a sub-region ("Côtes de Beaune"), which itself is below a village appellation ("Vosnes-Romanée"). At the top are *Premier Cru* wines, named after a village and a vineyard ("Volnay-Santenots") and *Grand Cru* wines which are labeled by the vineyard alone ("Romanée-Conti"). There are 31 Grand Cru vinyards in Burgundy proper. They are listed in Appendix D.

Thus, the wine from a particular vineyard may be a Grand Cru or Premier Cru, while the wine from other vineyards in the same village are blended and sold as a village appellation. Wines from lesser vineyards, blended this time with wines from elsewhere in Burgundy, will be sold as "Burgundy."

⊘In Bordeaux, the ridiculously complicated and outdated classifications (Appendix B) make it harder to navigate through the maze of labels. The cultivar is normally not mentioned on the label, as everybody is supposed to know that a red wine from Burgundy is a Pinot Noir; a wine from Pomerol is mostly Merlot; and that most Champagnes are blends of Pinot Noir and Chardonnay. The exception to the rule is Alsace, where labels often indicate the cultivar.

The mandatory inscriptions on French wine labels are the geographical name, the words "Appellation d'Origine Contrôlée" or "AOC" if the wine is ranked as such,[46] the name and address of the person responsible, and the volume of wine in the bottle. Any additional writing is unregulated and up to the producer. In particular, specifying the vintage year is not mandatory, although it is almost always done. The 1935 laws have been amended many times, to update the rules and define new AOC regions.

---

46. Champagnes are always AOC wines, but do not have to mention it on the label.

The VDQS (*Vin Delimité de Qualité Supérieure*) appellation is created in 1949; the VDQS wines are in an intermediate category between AOC and the lesser *Vin de Pays* and *Vin de Table* categories. Similar geographical delimitations and quality controls are or have since been introduced in other countries.

Italy, Spain, and Portugal

Italian winemakers have been falling behind in terms of technology since the 1600s. Bottles and other innovations reach Italy later than elsewhere. The overall quality of wines is low. The Italians sometimes refer to this long period of stagnation as *decadenza*. When Italy is unified in 1861, the march toward progress finally begins. But mildew and phylloxera soon arrive and ravage the vineyards. The big economic boom and the renaissance of Italian wines are delayed until after World War II.

Spain produces many wines since the 1600s, but the only ones good enough for export are in the south, near Jerez and Malaga. These wines are kept in "butts," oak barrels with a capacity of about 170 gallons.[47] Most of these wines are exported to England. In the rest of Spain, the level of technology is low. Wine is made in crude earthenware (*tinajas*) and stored in pigskins sealed with pitch and resin.

The Peninsular Wars (1808-1814) devastate the country. French troops pillage the sherry bodegas. After Napoleon's defeat, rebuilding takes place with remarkable success. The exports increase to 70,000 butts of sherry in 1873, the peak of exports until past World War II. In 1850, a railroad links Jerez to the north of Spain.

Powdery mildew arrives in 1850, but phylloxera reaches Jerez quite late, in 1894, and Rioja even later, in 1901. This is about 30 years after Bordeaux. These 30 years are a blessing for the wine regions of Rioja and Navarra. Their wines are sold for a good price to Bordeaux growers, who mix them with the few wines they are able to produce themselves, and then sell the blend as pure Bordeaux. In order to increase the quality of these questionable imports, the Bordeaux winemakers bring much-needed expertise, technology, and capital investment to northern Spain. Among other innovations, the Spanish *barrica* (a 59 gallon oak cask) is introduced from Bordeaux at the time.

Official delimitations and quality controls for wines of origin are established in 1933, the DO (denomination of origin) system, similar to the French AOC, starting in Rioja. Jerez and Malaga follow in 1935. During the Civil War, the vineyards are neglected and many wineries destroyed. The nationalist victory brings Generalissimo Franco to power in 1939.

The status of Portuguese wines until the onset of World War II is comparable to that of Spanish of Italian wines at the time, with the exception of Ports.

---

47. The "shipping butt" is 20% smaller.

Several government agencies are created in the 1930, the goals of which are to regulate every aspect of the port business, from vineyards to shipping. Port wines become the most regulated and controlled wines in the world. They still are today.

The *Casa Do Douro*, created in 1932 as assignment of the Federacy of the Grape growers of the Region of the Douro, is located in Régua in the Douro Valley. It is in charge of controlling and ranking vineyards. Twelve criteria determine the ranking of every vineyard in the Upper Douro. The rankings are based on criteria such as the precise location of the vineyard, its altitude, slope and exposure, the cultivars, the density of vines, their age, etc. It is illegal to irrigate the vineyards even in periods of severe drought. The ranking, from A to F, determine how much of the wine produced from a given vineyards is allowed to become Port. A-ranked vineyards may turn 100% of their wine into Port, while F-ranked vineyards are not allowed to produce any port at all. Their wine is often distilled to produced the brandy (*aguardente*) used in the Port-making process. The *Instituto do Vinho do Porto*[48] is created in 1933. It determines the annual production, controls the blending and aging of Ports, as well as all the aspects of shipping. These new regulations are aimed at enforcing and guaranteeing the quality of the wine. The true success of these measures will be measured well after the end of World War II.

---

48. Today, it is called the *Instituto dos Vinhos do Douro e do Porto.*

CHAPTER 5. FROM THE RENAISSANCE TO WORLD WAR II: THE NEW WORLDS

Although man is already ninety percent water, the prohibitionists are not yet satisfied.
—John Kendrick Bangs (1862-1922)

Christopher Columbus (1451?–1506) leaves Palos[1] for America in 1492. This is the first of his four trans-Atlantic voyages: 1492-3, 1493-6, 1498, and 1502-4. Columbus believes he is on his way to the East coast of India. He stops in the (Spanish) Canary Islands on his first, second, and fourth trip. The sweet Malvasia wines produced there are one reason. On his third trip, however, he stops at Funchal, in Madeira. Another adventurer, Amerigo Vespucci, makes several exploratory trips to Central and South America as well. In 1507, the German mapmaker Martin Waldseemuller, believing that Amerigo is actually the first to reach the New World, label the new lands "America" on a map in 1507. The name stuck.

In 1494, under the arbitration of Pope Alexander VI, a Spaniard, Spain and Portugal divide the New World among themselves at the Treaty of Tordesillas. All newly discovered land west of a line of longitude 370 leagues west of Cape Verde Islands is Spanish, and the rest Portuguese. Spain ratifies the treaty in July and Portugal in September. In 1498, the Portuguese Vasco de Gama (1469-1524) rounds the Cape of Good Hope (South Africa). An excitement for exploration, Christianization, and treasures from the new lands engulfs the western world.

---

1. Palos is a Spanish harbor on the Pacific Ocean.

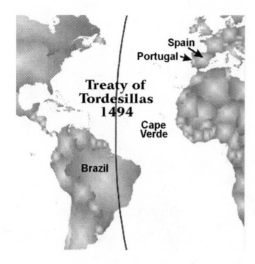

Figure 70: *By the treaty of Tordesillas, the New World is divided between Spain, west of the line, and Portugal, east of it (map: Kristin Reid).*

Columbus is followed by Conquistadores in search of gold, in particular Hernán Cortés who conquers Mexico from the Aztecs and Francisco Pizarro who defeats the Inca Empire in Peru. They are accompanied by Franciscan monks who bring with them cuttings and seeds of various *v. vinifera* cultivars. They need a little sacramental wine for Mass, and more for everyday drinking. The monks select hardy cultivars to maximize their chance of survival in new environments. Their principal white grape is probably the Muscat Alexandria. Nobody knows for sure what their principal red cultivar was, but the Spanish/Sardinian Monica is a plausible candidate. Its wine is not very good, but the vine itself is resilient and produces large quantities of grapes. The red cultivar becomes known as *Negra Corriente* in Peru, *País* in Chile, *Criolla* in Argentina, and *Mission* in California, where some of it still grows today.

At the time, no *v. vinifera* grows outside of Europe and the Near East. A dozen species of wild vines are native to the Atlantic coast of North America (*v. labrusca, v. rupestris, v. riparia*, etc.) but no wild vines bearing sweet grapes grow in the Southern Hemisphere. Thus, fifteen centuries after the Phoenicians, Greeks, and Romans bring viticulture from the shores of the Mediterranean Sea to continental Europe, *v. vinifera* finally takes on the world. This begins in Central America, spreads throughout South America, then south Texas and California. Independently, vines make their way to the Eastern United States, South Africa, then Australia and New Zealand.

CENTRAL AND SOUTH AMERICA

The journey of *vitis vinifera* from Europe to Central and South America begins in Mexico, goes south to Peru, Bolivia, Chile, Argentina, Uruguay, and finally reaches Brazil. The story of this journey and the key players involved are discussed by De Blij.[2] The first vineyards are planted near missions or churches.

The locations are not always ideal for viticulture, although some of the original locations are commercial enterprises today.

Hernán Cortés plants the first vines of the New Worlds in Mexico in 1522. In 1524, as governor of New Spain, he orders that any Spaniard with a land grant plant 1,000 vines per year for each 100 Indian slaves employed, every year for five years. This quickly ensures a large local production and, within a few years, the New World stops importing wines from the Old. Planting vineyards is done quickly almost everywhere the explorers go. In order to arrive on the Pacific side of South America, European wines must cross the Atlantic, be hauled overland through Panama, and then be reloaded on ships. It is much simpler to produce the wines locally.

In 1540, Bartolomeu de Terrazas plants vines in Cuzco, Peru, and then Hernando de Montenegro brings them to Lima and from there to Chile where grapevines grow in 1551. Pizarro also plants in Peru in 1547, after defeating the Incas. In 1566, Francesco de Carabantes plants a vineyard in the oasis of Ica in the coastal desert of Peru, 160 miles south of Lima and 30 miles from the coast. The Tacama Vineyards — Ica Valley — still produce wines today. In the 1560s, Peru has about 100,000 acres of vines, and its wines are exported throughout South America.

De Terrazas and de Carabantes also plant vines in what is today northern Chile. Diego Garcia de Cárceres plant vines at a much better location, near Santiago in 1554. In 1557, Father Pablo Cedron takes vines from Chile across the Andes to Mendoza, Argentina. The first vineyards in Chile's Central Valley are planted on the Andean foothills near San Juan, a city founded in 1562 by Juan Jufré y Montesa, governor of the captaincy general of Cuyo. This region includes San Juan, San Luis, and Mendoza — today's heart of Argentina's wine production. In 1626, the Jesuit Rocque Gonzáles de Santa Cruz[3] establishes the mission of Santa Cruz do Sol in the southernmost corner of Brazil. He is the first non-native person to enter the region. He is assassinated in 1628.

Thus, many of the early vineyards in Central and South America are originally planted for religious reasons, first by Franciscans, and then by Jesuits.[4] But wines are soon produced by secular estates. They are sold to European soldiers and settlers. Within a few years, the vineyards of South America are producing not only enough wines for all the local needs but also for occasional exports to Spain, to the dismay of the Spanish growers who hoped to increase their own exports instead. In 1595, King Philip II orders restrictions on the wine production in "New Spain" to protect wine producers in Spain. His order is widely ignored.

---

2. Harm Jan de Blij, *Wine Regions of the Southern Hemisphere* (Rowman & Allanheld, New Jersey, 1985).

3. He is now a saint. Pope John Paul II canonizes him in 1988.

4. The Society of Jesus is founded in 1540 by Saint Ignatius Loyola.

The thought of independence from Spanish or Portuguese colonial rule is present in people's minds throughout Central and South America. The catalyst is the Revolutionary War of the American Colonies against England (1775–1783). The first attempt at independence in South America follows Napoleon's invasion of Spain in 1808. It takes eleven years until Simon Bolivar ends Spanish rule in today's Colombia, Venezuela, Panama and Ecuador.

The liberator of Chile is Bernardo O'Higgins (1778–1842), the son of Spain's governor for Chile and viceroy for Peru. When Chile rebels against Spain in 1810, he joins the revolutionary forces. The Spaniards are driven out, but a new Spanish force invades Chile. O'Higgins becomes commander of the revolutionary army. Despite a heroic fight, he is defeated in 1814 at Rancagua, the capital city of Cachapoal, south of Santiago. O'Higgins and 120 of his fighters find refuge in the cellars of Santa Rita, near Santiago. In memory of this event, many Santa Rita wines have the number 120 on their label. O'Higgins flees to Argentina but returns in 1817 and joins forces with San Martin. The battles of Chacabuco and Maipo secure Chilean independence. After San Martin refuses the offer, General O'Higgins becomes the first dictator of Chile. He is a liberal dictator, the first in the Americas to abolish black slavery. Exiled from Chile, he dies in Peru, in 1842.

Figure 71: The "120" label on one of the best Santa Rita wines recounts the battle of Rancagua (courtesy: Santa Rita Winery).

On the east coast of South America, the liberator is José de San Martin (1778-1850), the son of a Spanish Governor in Argentina. After fighting Napoleon's army in Spain in 1808, he returns to Buenos Aires and enlists on the side of the revolutionaries. With his cavalry, the Mounted Grenadiers, he defeats a Spanish army in San Lorenzo, and then manages to cross the Andes into Chile to take on the city of Lima — center of Spanish power — from the west. After one loss, the combined Argentine-

Chilean army defeats the Spanish at the battle of Maipu. San Martin is considered to be the liberator of Argentina, Chile, and Peru.

The Portuguese colony of Brazil gains its independence without bloodshed. When Napoleon invades Portugal in 1807, King John VI and the whole royal family flee to Brazil, accompanied by an escort of British ships. Brazil becomes a kingdom of equal status with Portugal, with its capital in Rio de Janeiro. John returns to Portugal in 1821 and leaves his elder son Pedro as regent. When cries for independence become louder, Pedro demands independence from his father (who agrees) and declares himself Emperor Pedro I. He might have been happier becoming Sr. Pedro, or just Pedro. Unpopular, he ends up returning to Portugal in 1826 as King Pedro IV.

Free from European oversight and taxation, the new countries in Central and South America can now benefit from trade. Commercial winemaking in Chile starts in the 1700s, as Portuguese immigrants bring various cultivars, and experiment with the Isabella, a *vinifera x labrusca* hybrid. Although vineyards are planted in many locations, the technology remains primitive and the transportation difficult. For the most part, the production remains small and the trade localized. And the production still consist mostly of the undistinguished Mission (in red) and of the Muscat Alexandria (in white). Argentina, Chile, and Brazil are still a long way from being able to compete on the world market.

Don Silvestre Ochagavia Echazarreta is considered to be the founding father of the wine industry in Chile. In 1851, he brings from France cuttings of noble cultivars to plant on his land in Talagante. These include Cabernet Sauvignon, Merlot, Pinot Noir, Malbec, Chardonnay, Sauvignon, Semillon and Riesling. These pre-phylloxera vines still thrive in Chile. Echazarreta also convinces French growers and winemakers to come to Central Chile. At about the same time, immigrants from Italy, Switzerland and Germany start their own commercial vineyards.

Chile escapes the world-wide devastation brought by powdery mildew and phylloxera at the end of the 19th century. It is now the only country in the world where shoots can be planted directly into the ground, without grafting on American rootstock. But Argentina and Peru are affected. Their production plummets. The growing conditions in Chile are remarkably good. A vineyard sometimes produces two crops a year. However, for many years, the reputation of Chilean wines remains one of "plentiful and cheap." The production and export of high-quality wines dates back to the last decades of the 20th century.

In Argentina, the wine production is limited to the Criolla until the 1820s. After José de San Martin frees the country from Spanish colonial rule, a first wave of immigrants arrives from Italy, France and Spain. They bring with them European cultivars as well as knowledge of viticulture. Don Tiburcio Benegas settles in Mendoza in 1865. He imports cuttings from Chile and France, plants vineyards on his estate in San Vicenze, and starts the El Trapiche winery in 1883. More importantly, he lobbies to extend the national railroad system from Buenos

Aires to Mendoza. The railroad is inaugurated in 1885. This allows the marketing of Mendoza wines beyond the region of production and facilitates the immigration of Europeans. A second wave of immigration, mostly from Italy, brings Italian cultivars, such as the Bonarda, Barbera, and Trebbiano. Viticulture grows. However, the low level of investment slows the technological progress and the political situation severely limits the export market until long after World War II.

The development of viticulture in Brazil is even slower. The vineyards near Santa Cruz suffer from disease, fungi and rot. In the 1830s, the Isabella, a *labrusca × vinifera* hybrid is planted. It provides some resistance to disease but its wine is not of good quality. It is only in the 1870s that Italian immigrants find appropriate locations for planting *v. vinifera*, some 60 miles north of Porto Alegre, today the center of the Brazilian wine industry.

The first impact of Brazil on the history of wine is... sugar. Until slave labor is brought to Brazil, the world's largest sugar producer is (Portugal's) Madeira.[5] This group of volcanic islands is located in the Atlantic, some 350 west of Morocco and 300 miles north of the Canary Islands. Although the Madeira Islands are shown on navigation maps as early as the 1350s, they are not inhabited until being accidentally (re)discovered around 1420 by two captains of Prince Henry the Navigator, João Gonçalves Zarco and Tristão Vaz Teixeira. They seek refuge there after being blown off course by a storm.

Madeira is colonized by Portugal the following year. Various crops are planted, including wines and sugar cane, and timber exported back to Portugal. Madeira wines of good quality are already produced by 1455. It is possible that some of today's cultivars are planted at that time. Madeira is best known for its sugar, until the cheap Brazilian sugar supplants Madeira's production in the 1500s. The sugar canes are pulled out and more vines planted. In the early days, much of the wine produced in Madeira is acidic, and is not fortified. As barrels ("pipes") of this wine are shipped from Madeira to South America or the Far East via the tip of South Africa, they cross the tropics and the equator and are exposed to warm temperatures for extended periods of time. Interestingly, this substantially improve Madeira wines. By the 1700s, ships routinely have pipes of Madeira wine as ballast.

Since the 1800s, the Madeira wine is fortified with grape alcohol. In order to reproduce the temperatures to which the wine would be exposed during sea trips, the *estufa* (stove) system is invented. The wine is kept for months at about 120F or more. Stainless steel containers with hot-water pipes running through them are used for the common Madeira. After that treatment, the wine is kept in barrels for several years. The better wines never spend time in stainless steel. Instead, they are kept in large wooden casks in a heated room. The best wines are kept for years on the roof or under the eaves of lodges, exposed to the summer heat (the "canteiro" method). In the late 1800s, downy mildew and then

---

5. P. Russell, *Prince Henry "The Navigator," a Life* (Yale University Press, New Haven, 2001).

phylloxera destroy most of the vineyards. American-European hybrid cultivars are planted, and the quality of the wine falls. For over a century, the reputation of Madeira wines is low.

The recovery begins in the 1970s. Today, most of the common Madeira wine is made with the Tinta Negra Mole cultivar, and mass-processed in estufas. The quality varies. The best Madeira[6] wines are aged 5, 10 or 15 years in casks and labeled by the noble cultivar used: Malmsey, Boal, Verdelho, or Sercial. The rare "vintaged" Madeira spends over 20 years in casks, some of them much longer. Many of these wines then spend time in large glass demi-johns[7] before being bottled. Once bottled, a Madeira wine survives almost forever. The sweetest Madeira is made from the Malmsey, which grows in the lowest elevations on the southern coast of the islands. The dryer Bual is at higher altitudes and the Verdhelo on the cooler north side. The driest and most acidic of the noble cultivars in Madeira, Sercial (a.k.a. "bitter enough to choke a dog"), is planted up to 1,000 meters above sea level. Yet, its wine becomes surprisingly delicate after 10 years in wood.

UNITED STATES[8]

The East

A dozen[9] wild vine species are native to the Eastern coast of North America: *v. rotundifolia, munsonioana, riparia, labrusca, rupestris, aestivalis*, etc. The fruits of these native species contain less sugar as *v. vinifera*. Their wines are not of good quality, although wines have been made with them (and still are). However, many of these species have at least some resistance to phylloxera, mildew, and various diseases. *V. vinifera* is very vulnerable. It is virtually impossible to produce wine in the East of the United States from imported European cultivars, unless grafted onto American rootstock, something that is not known until the late 19th century. Short of grafting, there is no choice but to use native vines or hybrids to produce wine. The story of the early wines of the East Coast

---

6. The solera system, discussed in the next chapter, is no longer in use in Madeira. Old "Madeira Solera" wines are still occasionally found, but the date on the bottle is not a vintage year. It refers to the year the solera was started.
7. The capacity of a demi-john is about six gallons.
8. See T. Pinney, *A History of Wine in America: From the Beginnings to Prohibition* (University of California Press, Berkeley, 1985) and *A History of Wine in America: From Prohibition to the Present* (University of California Press, Berkeley, 2005).
9. The precise number of native species is a matter of debate since most of them easily hybridize.

of the United States is that of many failed attempts, sometimes by famous people.

Figures 72-73: v. riparia, left, and v. labrusca, right (photo SKE).

When Europeans arrive in North America, they often bring with them cuttings of *v. vinifera*. In the 1560s, French Huguenots arrive in Florida, near the current location of Jacksonville. They may be the first to make wine in the continental United States, but probably from *v. rotundifolia*. In 1569, Spaniards arrive in South Carolina and also try to make wine, without success. Lord Delaware imports 10,000 cuttings from France and plants them in Virginia in 1619. All his plants die, as do those of Lord Baltimore who plants 200 acres of vines in 1662, and those of William Penn in 1682. German immigrants unsuccessfully try to grow *v. vinifera* in Germantown. Greeks, Italians, French and Spaniards try their luck from Spanish Florida to French Louisiana... The vines die from phylloxera or fungal diseases.

Thomas Jefferson (1743-1826) is one of the most famous wine lovers in American history.[10] In the early 1770s, he convinces the Italian Filippo Mazzei to import European cultivars and start a commercial winery on 200 acres near his own estate at Monticello. No wine is produced. The experiment stops at the onset of the Revolutionary War (1775-1783). Jefferson's own experiments with *v. vinifera* at Monticello fail as well. He refers to them as the "parents of misery."

---

10. J.M. Gabler, *The Wines and Travels of Thomas Jefferson* (Bacchus Press, Baltimore, 1995); J. Harrington, *The Cultivated Life: Thomas Jefferson and Wine* (PBS, 2005).

Figures 74-75: v. rupestris (left) and the Isabella, a labrusca ×vinifera hybrid
(right: photo SKE).

Figure 76: Thomas Jefferson (1743-1826), 3rd President and wine
lover (painting by Gilbert Stuart, courtesy: constitution.org).

After the death of his wife Martha, Jefferson accepts
the position of Commissioner in France, where he serves
from 1784 to 1789. After spending three years in Paris, Jefferson visits many wine-growing regions in France,
Germany and Italy, and selects wines for George Washington's Presidential cellar.[11] In the Bordeaux region, he is
enthusiastic about Château Haut-Brion, and falls in love with the noble-rot wine
of Chateau d'Yquem. He takes cuttings from Yquem with him back to Virginia.
They all die. He tries again, and even imports barrels of French soil with the cuttings. The vines die. For nearly 30 years he plants French, Italian and German
vines at Monticello. He remains convinced that wines as good as the best French
wines can be produced in the US.

---

11. Jefferson's favorite wine "without a single exception" is the Hermitage Blanc, a blend
of Marsanne and Roussanne cultivars from the famous Hermitage vineyard, north of
the city of Valence in northern Côtes du Rhône.

Jefferson believes that wine is a much healthier and more civilized beverage than the strong distilled liquors widely consumed at the time. During his tenure as President (1801-1809), he promotes wine: "No nation is drunken where wine is cheap; and none sober where the dearness of wine substitutes ardent spirits as the common beverage." He wants to keep wine taxes low, hoping to transform America into a nation of wine drinkers.

Around 1740, James Alexander discovers an accidental hybrid of *v. labrusca* and *v. vinifera*, not far from the location where William Penn had planted his European cuttings. He names it the "Alexander." This hybrid provides good resistance to pests and diseases, and produces a decent wine. It is used to make wine commercially in Indiana, in the early 1800s.

Experimentation with American-European hybrids[12] produces a range of cultivars, such as the Isabella (*v. labrusca* ×*v. vinifera*) and the Delaware (*v. labrusca* ×*v. aestivalis* ×*v. vinifera*). Other wineries rely on native vines such as the Concord or the Clinton, both *v. labrusca*. The flavor of the wines obtained from hybrids or native cultivars is often described as "musky" or "foxy." The wines never achieve the quality expected from European imports.

A number of wineries achieve reasonable commercial success in the first half of the 19th century. They include Johann Schiller's winery in Cooksville (incorporated into Mississauga, Ontario, in 1967), which uses the Labrusca; the Pennsylvania Wine Company, established near Philadelphia, produces wine from the Alexander; in 1813, Nicholas Longworth, a self-made millionaire from Cincinnati, plants the Alexander grape on the banks of the Ohio River near Cincinnati. He first produces a fortified wine that "resembles Madeira." Then, he experiments with the Catawba and discovers that the foxy taste comes from the skin of the berry. He separates the skins from the must and produces a decent but light-colored wine. Finally, after breaking a great many bottles, he becomes successful with a sparkling wine, the "Catawba Champagne." Ohio is the largest producer of wine in North America in the 1850s. But the business collapses in 1859, when black rot attacks the vines.

Other wineries are found around Hermann, Missouri and near the Finger Lakes in New York State. The Concord grape grows in New Hampshire, where it makes much better jelly than wine. Muscadine (*v. rotundifolia*) wine is made in Carolina and Georgia. The wine industry is also found near the cooler shores of Lake Erie, reducing the problems associated with rot and fungi. The most successful vines there are the so-called "French hybrids": Maréchal Foch (*v. ruparia* × *v. rupestris* ×*v. vinifera*), Seyval Blanc (a hybrid of hybrids) and others.

All these wineries suffer from the low quality of the wines they produce as compared to wines made in Europe from *v. vinifera* cultivars. Other problems include fungi and diseases, the Civil War, and then the Temperance movement

---

12. This experimentation takes place long before the monk Gregor Mendel (1822-1884) publishes the results of his experiments on genetics, in 1866.

and Prohibition. Thus, even though the first US wines are produced on the East Coast, they are not made of *v. vinifera* grapes.[13] The production of quality wines east of the Rockies begins in the 20th century.

The Southwest

In the Southwest, *v. vinifera* arrives from Mexico with Franciscan Friars. The first vineyard is planted in 1682 in Ysleta, along the Rio Grande, today part of the city of El Paso.[14] This is not very far north from the winery and distillery at Parras de la Fuentes,[15] established in 1597 by Don Lorenzo Garciá and still in operation today. Although Spanish missionaries are growing vines in Baja California (Mexico) as early as the 1670s, it takes another century for vines to reach California itself.

In 1769, the now "blessed" Father Junipero Serra (1703-1784) brings the *Mission* grape from Mexico to San Diego. He is a tough Friar. He forcibly converts the Indians to Christianity and uses them as laborers. He establishes nine of the 21 missions in California, from San Diego to Sonoma[16]. The first California wine is drunk in 1772 in Monterey, at the Mission of San Carlo Borromeo, where Junipero Serra is buried. In the 1790s, the San Gabriel mission near Los Angeles produces some 35 million gallons of wine, as well as brandy. In 1823, the Mexican Revolution ends Spanish rule. In 1833, the Mexico secularizes the missions, causing consternation and great anger among the Jesuits. After losing the US-Mexican war (1846-1847), Mexico is forced to sell to the United States its territories from the Rio Grande to California.

Until the 19th century, most of California's vineyards grow the Mission grape and the level of technology is low. This improves mid-century, starting in the Pueblo of Los Angeles. The total population in 1860 is less than 4,500, of which almost 10% are French. In 1866 Jullien[17] notes that most of the California vineyards are in Los Angeles county. They produce some 500,000 gallons of low-quality wine annually. The first to plant a vineyard is Louis Bouchet, in 1827. He

---

13. Today, one can still find wines made from various American native grapes (catawba, muscadine, norton) as well as hybrids (chambourcin, seyval blanc, vignoles).
14. The oldest *commercial* winery in Texas, Val Verde in Del Rio, is established in 1883.
15. It is about 100 miles west of Monterrey, in the state of Coahuila which borders the state of Texas.
16. From south to north, they are: San Diego de Alcala, San Luis Rey de Francia, San Juan Capistrano, San Gabriel, San Fernando Rey de España, San Buenaventura, Santa Barbara, Santa Ines, La Purisima Conception, San Luis Obispo de Tolosa, San Miguel, San Antonio de Padua, Nuestra Señora de la Soledad, San Carlos Borromeo, San Juan Bautista, Santa Cruz, Santa Clara de Asis, San Jose, San Francisco de Asis, San Rafael, and San Francisco Solano.
17. A. Jullien, *Topographie de tous les vignobles connus* (Slatkine, Genève, 1985, reprint of the 1866 Paris edition).

is also a barrel-maker. In 1832, Jean-Louis Vignes[18] buys a ranch and imports *v. vinifera* cuttings which he grafts onto Mission rootstock. He is the first to produce wine of quality comparable to French wine. In 1849, the Gold Rush results in a massive increase in the population of the West Coast.[19] Among the immigrants are the Hungarian Agoston Haraszthy, the Germans Charles Krug and Jacob Beringer, and the Frenchmen Paul Masson and Charles Lefranc. Lefranc plants French cultivars at the Almadén vineyards in 1857. Krug is the first to make wine in Napa Valley in 1858, near St. Helena. By the late 1800s, there are over 400 vineyards in Napa.

The most important and colorful hero of viticulture in California is Agoston Haraszthy (1812-1869). He arrives in San Diego (population 650) in 1849 and plants fruit trees. He gets involved in politics and is elected sheriff in 1859. Elected to the State Assembly, he moves to the Bay area. After getting involved in gold and silver refining and other enterprises, he establishes a winery in Sonoma valley in 1857, Szeptaj Estate (now Buena Vista). Haraszthy's most critical contribution to California wine is his trip to Europe in 1861 and the sub-sequent import of nearly 100,000 vine shoots representing some 1,400 European cultivars. Among them might have been the *Zinfandel*. Haraszthy never receives the promised payment from the Governor for the European trip and the vine shoots, but vines spread throughout California from his nurseries. In 1862, he publishes an account of his trips and advice on viticulture in "Grape Culture, Wine and Wine-Making with Notes upon Agriculture and Horticulture."

There has been much speculation about the origin of the Zinfandel. The mystery is now elucidated, owing to the research of Carole Meredith and co-workers,[20] specialists in DNA and the genealogy of grapes. Following several trips to Croatia, they have established unambiguously that Zinfandel is an ancient cultivar from the Dalmatian coast, locally named *Crljenak Kastelanski*. The Italian *Primitivo* cultivar, incorrectly believed to be (and often marketed as) the "father of the Zinfandel," is in fact one of its descendents.

Until the trans-continental railroad is finished in 1869, the wines produced in California are consumed locally. Transporting them across the Rocky Mountains or around the tip of South America is too costly, long, and difficult. As soon as rail transport becomes possible, *v. vinifera* wines from California make their way to the East Coast. However, many wines arrived spoiled and the cost of transportation renders California wines almost as expensive as European wines shipped across the Atlantic. A large fraction of the wines produced in California are distilled into brandy. However, phylloxera arrives with the new railroad. The

---

18. In French, "vignes" means vines.
19. The population of California jumps from some 14,000 in 1848 to almost 250,000 in 1852.
20. C.P. Meredith, *Science as a window into wine history* (1863rd Stated Meeting report, winter 2003), p. 54. Dr. Meredith is now retired from U.C. Davis.

pest destroys most of the vineyards. The wonderful Carneros district north of San Francisco is particularly hard hit. Grafting *vinifera* onto resistant American rootstock saves the wine industry.

Figure 77: Agoston Haraszthy around 1850, then Sheriff of San Diego County (© San Diego Historical Society).

In the 1880s, California surpasses Ohio as the leading wine-producing state. Universities become involved in the study of wines and viticulture. This begins at the University of California (UC) Berkeley, and then moves to UC Davis, today's leading US university in the area of viticulture. In 1894, the California Wine Association is created. It controls a large fraction of the production. At the 1900 World Exhibition in Paris, Californian wines win numerous awards. Few people notice. The 1906 San Francisco earthquake destroys or ruins many wineries. Yet, this is nothing compared to the devastation that Prohibition brings to the wine industry.

TEMPERANCE AND PROHIBITION

The societal changes that follow the Industrial Revolution include an increase in the population of cities by poor working-class people. Overcrowding and poverty are factors in the increased incidence of drunkenness, domestic violence, and crime.[21] The general belief is that reducing or eliminating the consumption of alcohol will cure or at least alleviate these problems. One could argue that alcohol abuse is a consequence, not a cause, of the problem. However, it is much cheaper to control alcohol consumption than to provide decent housing, schooling, and wages. Starting in the 1800s, temperance movements appear in many countries. Their initial goal is to reduce alcoholism rather than prohibit the consumption of distilled or fermented beverages. The temperance movements are often supported by Churches. Various governments react differently to the demands of (some of) their constituents. The general misery that follows World War I, especially in Europe, results in even more widespread

---

21. England suffers from social breakdown during the "gin craze" in the late 17th and early 18th centuries. Gin is grain alcohol flavored with oil from juniper berries. It is invented in 1650 by the French physician Franciscus de la Boie, who uses it as a diuretic. The French word for "juniper" is "genièvre," which to the British sounds like "Genève" (Geneva, in English). The word "gin" is "Geneva" abbreviated. See P. Dillon, *Gin: The Much-Lamented Death of Madam Geneva* (Justin, Charles, & Co., Boston, 2003).

alcohol abuse which compels many nations to limit in various ways and some-times prohibit alcohol consumption.

The earliest temperance societies appear in Connecticut in 1789, following Dr. Benjamin Rush's arguments about the evil consequences of alcohol con-sumption. Similar societies soon appear in Virginia, New York, and other states. Temperance movements also exist in the Netherlands and Canada (since the early 1800s), England, Australia and Norway (since the early 1830s), Denmark (since 1864), New Zealand (since the 1890s), and other countries, with the exception of France. Prohibition is imposed in Russia from 1914 to 1925, Iceland from 1915 to 1922, Norway from 1916 to 1927, and Finland from 1919 to 1932. Many laws first enacted during that period are still in effect, especially in Northern Europe and the US. These regulate and heavily tax the sale of beer, wine and hard liquors, dictate days and times when alcohol can be consumed in bars, etc.

In the US, temperance societies evolve into abstinence societies, often pro-moting a complete prohibition of alcohol consumption. In 1826, the national American Temperance Society is created. Soon, it has chapters in all the states, often with the support of local Protestant Churches. By the mid 19th century, there is an Anti-Saloon League and a Prohibition Party. Prohibition becomes a major topic of debate during political campaigns. The state of Maine enacts Pro-hibition in 1851. The American Civil War (1861-1865) relegates these issues to the back burner, but they return in force soon after the war ends. The fight for legally enforced Prohibition continues at the local, state, and federal levels. More and more states prohibit alcohol: three in 1905, nine in 1912, twenty-six (of 48) in 1916.

On January 16, 1920, the 18th Amendment to the US Constitution (Vol-stead Act) becomes the law of the land. With allowances for private, medical or sacramental use, it is illegal to "manufacture, sell, barter, transport, import, export, furnish or possess intoxicating liquors." The word "consume" is not men-tioned. "Intoxicating" is defined as exceeding 0.5% alcohol per volume, a mere 1 proof. Prohibition[22] is now the law of the land.

Making alcohol illegal is a social experiment doomed to fail. It makes outlaws of a majority of otherwise law-abiding citizens, promotes contempt for the law, greatly increases organized crime, and generates corruption on a massive scale. Another unintended consequence is the rash of blindness and death from drinking methanol,[23] the simplest of all alcohols also known as "wood alcohol": CH_3OH. It is estimated that over 50,000 people die from alcohol poisoning in the first eight years of Prohibition.

---

22. J.H. Timberlake, *Prohibition and the Progressive Movement* (Harvard University Press, Cambridge MA 1963); H. Peterson, *The Great Illusion: An Informal History of Prohibition* (Greenwood Press, New York, 1968); E. Behr, *Prohibition* (Arcade, New York, 1996).

Figure 78: Andrew John Volstead (1869-1947) around 1933, congressman of Minnesota and author of the disastrous Volstead Act (© Minnesota Historical Society).

By 1921, virtually the entire police force of Cincinnati is on the payroll of the famous bootlegger George Remus. There are over 5,000 "speakeasies"[24] in the US in 1922, and about 27,000 in 1927. During Prohibition, the number of homicides sharply increases,[25] as does the consumption of alcohol and distilled liquors.[26] The police also destroy the corn-alcohol stills used to make the ethanol which powers most automobiles and farm machinery. Petroleum replaces ethanol. President Harding, who votes for Prohibition as a Senator, keeps stocks of bootleg liquor in the White House. The internal contradictions of Prohibition are summarized by would-be poets, as in the following lines by an unknown author:

> When Christ turned water into wine
> There were no drys to scold and whine
> Today's prohibitors would rail
> And put the Son of God in jail.

The effects of Prohibition in the US and elsewhere on wine production and sales are enormous all around the world. Between 1919 and 1925, the number of wineries in California falls from 700 to a little over 100 and the total US wine production drops from 55 to 3.5 million gallons. However, the acreage dedicated to table grapes doubles to 600,000 acres. After all, growing fruit is legal. For white grapes, the choice is the Thompson Seedless, developed by William Thompson. It is a prolific grape, unable to produce a decent wine. For red grapes, the choice is Zinfandel. This cultivar is amazingly productive unless the vine is old (say, over 30 years) or severely pruned.

---

23. Methanol or wood alcohol, commonly used in antifreeze and many solvents, is much more reactive than ethanol, the alcohol in wine. The metabolism of ethanol involves acetaldehyde and acetic acid (vinegar), while that of methanol involves the much more toxic formaldehyde and formic acid. Optical tissues are highly sensitive to formic acid (Sandy DasGupta, Texas Tech University).

24. One must "speak easy" to the doorman to be allowed into the underground bar.

25. Bureau of Census: *Historical Statistics of the United States: Colonial Times to 1970* (US Gov. Printing Office, 1975) part 1.

26. C. Warburton, *The Economic Results of Prohibition* (Columbia UP, New York, 1932).

Concentrated grape juice in a can is sold as Vine Glo[27] with instructions on how to ferment its contents. Packages of dehydrated grapes with a yeast pill are sold as Wine Bricks.[28] But this is all low-quality grape juice. Most premium cultivars disappear from California. Less than 100 acres of Cabernet Sauvignon survive Prohibition.

The 18th Amendment is repealed by the 21st Amendment, on December 5, 1933. But then, the country is deep in the Depression and wine has become an unfamiliar luxury. Some research is still being done at UC Davis, and the Wine Institute of California is still promoting wine, but the industry has a long way to go. The production of wines in states other than California has mostly disappeared. World War II temporarily stimulates the industry as imports from Europe plummet.

It takes decades for the wine industry in California to recover. Massive investments are needed to rebuild wineries, plant premium cultivars, educate the domestic customer, and develop a market for quality wines. By 1940, over 80% of the production consists of low-quality sweet or fortified wines. A few dry table wines are sold under generic names such as "Burgundy" or "Chablis," although the wines themselves bear no resemblance to the French Burgundy or Chablis.

On December 2, 1942, a team of physicists led by Enrico Fermi achieves the first controlled nuclear reaction in history, the fission of ^{235}U. The nuclear reactor, dubbed CP-1 for Chicago Pile 1, is built in a squash court under the stands of the football field at the University of Chicago. The reactor is shut down after 28 minutes of operation at 200 Watts. This experiment makes the Manhattan project possible. The nuclear age has begun. Eugene Wigner opens a bottle of Chianti to mark the event. Most members of the team sign it.

SOUTH AFRICA

In South Africa, v. vinifera is planted for commercial, not religious, reasons. The Dutch need to supply their ships on their way around the Cape to the Far East, where they buy spices. In the 1640s, the Dutch East India Company decides to establish a supplying post at the Cape of Good Hope. They appoint Jan van Riebeeck to lead the first settlers.[29] They arrive at the foot of Table Mountain in 1652. Van Riebeeck quickly realizes that the area is appropriate for viticulture, and orders a variety of v. vinifera shoots from France and Germany. They arrive in

---

27. *Time*, November 16, 1931.
28. *Time*, August 17, 1931.
29. Harm Jan de Blij, *Wine Regions of the Southern Hemisphere* (Rowman & Allanheld, New Jersey, 1985).

1655 and, in February 1659, "... wine is pressed for the first time from Cape grapes." In 1662, he is transferred to Java.

Figure 79: The bottle of Chianti signed by the scientists who performed the very first controlled nuclear reaction in history (courtesy of Argonne National Laboratory).

In 1679, the new governor of Cape Town is Simon Van der Stel (1639-1712). His father Adriaan van der Stel was Governor of Mauritius. Upon his arrival, Simon finds a flourishing viticulture, but the overall quality of the wines is low. He sets the first rules in South Africa aimed at improving the quality of the local wines, by compelling winegrowers to wait until the fruit is fully mature before harvesting. He also identifies the wine region of Stellenbosch, East of Cape Town; today the heart of South Africa's wine country. In 1685, he also purchases a large estate south of Cape Town, Constantia. He imports 100,000 shoots from Europe as well as the most modern winemaking equipment available. He produces a strong, sweet, and scented wine; the best South Africa has to offer for many years.

The Revocation of the Edict of Nantes in 1685 by Louis XIV — grandson of Henry IV, who had issued the Edict — sends the French protestants (Huguenots) fleeing the country. Some escape to Holland, and the Dutch convince 150 of them to start a new life in South Africa. They arrive in Cape Town in 1690, and settle in Stellenbosch, Paarl, and Franschhoek ("French Corner"). They bring with them cultivars new to South Africa as well as technological know-how. Simon Van der Stel retires in 1699 but stays in his Constantia estate, where he dies in 1712. His son Willam Adriaan takes over as Governor. He becomes a more controversial figure. In 1795, the British take control of the region and impose stricter quality standards. South Africa becomes a part of the British Empire in 1814, and England becomes the major market for South African wines.

Figure 80: Simon van der Stel, standing, and Willem Adriaan van der Stel, sitting on the horse (courtesy: Leo van der Stel and the Van der Stel family in Holland. The original painting by Jan Weenix, c. 1669, was damaged by fire. The reproduction is by Simon Balyon).

After Simon van der Stel's death, Constantia is divided and sold. The largest fraction of it, Groot Constantia, is acquired by the German Hendrik Cloete in 1778. He plants Frontignac (Muscat à Petits Grains), as well as Pontac, red and white Muscadel and some Chenin Blanc, locally known as Steen. These cultivars become the ingredients of the "Constantia" or "Vin de Constance." This is a late-harvest, but not Noble-Rot, wine. This wine maintains a glorious reputation for over a century. It is found at the court of kings, emperors and tsars. Napoleon is said to have insisted on having Constantia wine during his first exile. Louis Philippe, King of France, orders substantial quantities of it in 1833. But many of the other wines produced in South Africa at the time are of much lesser quality. The overall reputation of South African wines is mixed. Today, parts of the former Constantia estate are in Groot Constantia, Klein Constantia, Buitenverwachting, Constantia Uitsig, and Steenberg Estate, all of which produce remarkable wines.

Then events turn sour. Powdery mildew appears at the Cape in 1859. Wine production drops precipitously. In 1861, the Gladstone government removes the Empire's preferential tariffs. Exports to England, the main market for South African wines, drop. So do profits. In 1869, the discovery of gold and diamonds diamonds in Central South Africa causes a massive wave of immigration. The local market for grows, but phylloxera arrives in 1885. It devastates the vineyards. Constantia is ruined. Some of the vineyards are later replanted on American rootstock, but the Vin de Constance is gone for over a century.

Figure 81: An 1881 "Vin de Constance," bottled in 1883 (courtesy: Klein Constantia Winery).

At the end of World War I, the wine industry in South Africa still has not recovered. The KWV (Cooperative Winegrower's Association) is formed in 1918. It is legally empowered to limit production and set minimum prices. This stabilizes the market and pushes the industry into the modern era.

In 1925, the South African oenologist Abraham Perold, Professor at Stellenbosch University, creates a cross[30] of Pinot Noir, which is difficult to grow but produces very delicate wines, and Cinsaut (sometimes spelled Cinsault), which is much more prolific and sturdy. In South Africa at the time, Cinsaut is called Hermitage. The *Pinot Noir x Hermitage* cross, *Pinotage*, becomes the most distinct cultivar of South Africa. It has a good resistance to disease and can produce very powerful but also very delicate wines, the best of which age beautifully. It is sometimes referred to as the "South African Zinfandel." The Pinotage remains unique to South Africa until the late 1980s. It now grows in New Zealand, California, and a few other regions.

AUSTRALIA AND NEW ZEALAND

Captain Arthur Phillip leads the first fleet to Australia, as Governor of the new penal colony of Botany Bay on the east coast of the continent. He arrives in September, 1788 with cuttings from France, Germany and South Africa. He believes that the region is well-suited to the production of wine, and plants his cuttings in what are today the Royal Botanical Gardens in Sydney. The first two bunches of Australian grapes are picked there in January, 1791. However, they do not survive long. The climate is hot and humid, and the vines succumb to fungi and disease. Phillip plants again, this time some 16 miles north of Sydney, at a

---

30. A *cross* involves two (or more) cultivars within the same species, while a *hybrid* involves cultivars from different species. Pinot Noir and Cinsaut are both v. *vinifera*.

higher elevation. But he returns to England in 1792, and his vineyard fades away. Being a penal colony, most Europeans who live in Australia at the time are not of the social class used to consume wines. The local market for wine is virtually non-existent.

The first commercial winery is that of the explorer Gregory Blaxland. In 1817, he plants a vineyard using Cabernet Sauvignon cuttings from South Africa. His wines win medals in England in 1822. At about the same time, Captain John McArthur and his sons James and (especially) William establish a winery just thirty miles west of Sydney. Their wines also win prizes at competitions in England.

James Busby (1802-1871), a Scot who studied viticulture in France, arrives in Australia in 1824 with his parents.[31] He purchases 200 acres in the Hunter Valley and experiments with viticulture. In 1831 he travels throughout Europe and sends back to Australia thousands of cuttings from hundreds of European cultivars. This includes the Shiraz, a most important cultivar in Australia today. In 1833, before having produced any wine in Hunter Valley, Busby moves to New Zealand and plants vines in Waitangi, in the northern peninsula of North Island. Busby is not the first to grow vines in New Zealand. An Australian missionary, the Rev. Samuel Marsden, had planted vines at Kerikeri, also on the north-east coast of North Island, in 1819. But there is no evidence that he produced wine. James Busby is credited for making and selling the first New Zealand wine in 1835.

Among the immigrants who arrive in the early 1840s are two young doctors: Christopher Penfold and Henry Lindeman. Both of them study medicine at St. Bartholomew's Hospital in London; both believe in the medicinal virtues of wine; and they sail to South Australia with vine cuttings. Lindeman arrives in 1840, purchases a property near Gresford in New South Wales, and names it Cawarra. He plants red (Shiraz? — he names it "Cyras") and white (Roussanne? — he names it "Rousette") cultivars. The winery has since moved to Pokolbin but has remained in the hands of Lindeman's descendents. Penfold arrives in 1844, and establishes a practice on his estate, "The Grange," named after his wife Mary's home in England. He plants a vineyard are produces fortified wines for his patients. The Grange wine quickly earns a solid reputation and winemaking gradually replaces Penfold's medical practice. After Penfold's death in 1870, Mary, her daughter Georgina and her husband take over the business. Over the years, new vineyards are purchased and business grows. The main focus switches to table wines in the 1950, and today's Grange is one of the very best Australian wines.

The Australian Gold Rush of 1851 brings a huge wave of immigrants and ultimately results in the colonization of all the southern states. New vineyards

---

31. His father is appointed to evaluate the coal reserves and establish water supplies for Sydney.

and wineries are established, in particular in the Barossa and Hunter Valleys. By 1870, the production of Australian wines is a substantial 2.3 million gallons. It consists mostly of dry table wines from a comprehensive collection of *vinifera* cultivars, as well as fortified wines, often called Port or Sherry. In most of the early wineries, the grapes are treaded by foot. Widespread use of wine presses, oak barrels, and temperature controls dates to the late 19th century.

Powdery mildew strikes in 1876. Phylloxera is first detected at Phillip Bay in 1877. Only South Australia remained phylloxera-free. In the early 1890s, it hits New Zealand harder than Australia. Some winegrowers graft *v. vinifera* onto American rootstock; others grow the Isabella hybrid instead. By 1938, less than 200 acres of vineyards remain in New Zealand. As Australian wines struggle to recover, the (mostly British) market collapses as World War I is followed by waves of anti-alcohol sentiment and prohibition.

World War II is about to begin.

CHAPTER 6. MODERN WINES

Wine is the most civilized thing in the world.
— Ernest Hemingway (1899-1961)

For the entire century ending with World War II, viticulture endures a succession of catastrophes. They start in 1845 with the powdery mildew, which is ultimately controlled with chemicals. But then, phylloxera forces almost all the vineyards in the world to be replanted, with (selected) *v. vinifera* cultivars grafted onto American rootstock. As soon as the replanting is done and downy mildew is overcome, World War I brings general poverty and destruction. The Russian Revolution, Temperance and Prohibition, and then the Great Depression dramatically reduce the demand for fine wines all over the world. Then, World War II spreads another wave of destruction.

During this long period, many wineries go out of business. The ones that somehow survive badly need new infrastructure, that is investment, and markets. Reconstruction begins. It takes time. In Europe, in particular in France, the very ancient wine tradition speeds up the recovery of the wine industry. Wine is a priority. In California a complete overhaul is needed and the attitudes of the customer toward wine have to be changed. This requires investment and advertising. As for South America, South Africa, Australia and New Zealand, massive investments are needed to upgrade the technology and develop international markets. In many countries, the political situation discourages foreign (and domestic) investment. Their recovery is much slower.

FRANCE

Bordeaux

After World War II, the wines from Pomerol and St. Emilion begin their rise to prominence. The best wines from Graves are classified in 1953 (reds) and 1959 (whites). In contrast to the 1855 classification, which defined 1st through 5th growths, the Graves are simply ranked as "Classés" or not. In 1955, with a revision in 1996, the best St. Emilion wines are ranked. The categories are "Grands Crus Classés A," "Grands Crus Classés B" and "Grand Crus Classés." All the official classifications are given in Appendix B. The wines from Pomerol have yet to be classified, and they may never be. Thus *Pétrus*, arguably of the best Merlot in the world, is not classified.

Figures 82-83: Main wine regions of France (maps: Kristin Reid).

Some Médoc wines, absent from the 1855 Classification, are ranked as "Crus Bourgeois" (in 1996) and "Crus Artisans" (in 1997). One sometimes finds "Crus Grand Bourgeois" and "Grands Bourgeois Exceptionnels." These classifications are confusing. The average wine shopper needs substantial documentation when buying wine, and even then, looks can be deceiving. Since money and egos are involved, it is nearly impossible to update the classifications, something that is badly needed. An inspection of the 1855 Classification reveals that some chateaux no longer exist, others have substantially improved, and others yet deserve to be demoted. A new and impartial ranking of wines from Bordeaux and other wine regions has been proposed by Orley Ashenfelter.[1] His rankings (Appendix C) are based on the prices fetched by specific wines at auctions throughout the world.

Another "ranking" of sorts is the result of the influence of an American, Robert M. Parker Jr. and his 50-100 points system.[2] Parker points have sub-

---

1. O. Ashenfelter, *The Wine Educator* 1 (1), 3 (1989).

stantial influence on the retail value of wines, not just the wines from Bordeaux but from all over the world.[3] Parker's ability to taste and remember an incredible number of wines is truly remarkable. And Parker is to be credited or blamed for the emergence of the so-called "garage-wines" which often command very high prices. Critics note that the points reflect Parker's own taste rather than some absolute worth. Some winemakers are chemically "designing" wines[4] in order to produce a high Parker rating. One may also argue that the beauty is in the eye of the beholder, or rather the palate of the drinker. Many wines are interesting and for many different reasons.

Burgundy and Chablis

While Château-bottling is compulsory in Bordeaux for classified wines since 1972, the wines in Burgundy and Alsace are purchased in bulk by the *négociants* (shippers) who bottle it themselves. As a result, one needs to know not just the appellation of the wine and the vintage year, but the reputation of the shipper as well.

The Hospices de Beaune, the hospital founded by Nicolas Rolin in 1443, are famous for their wines and wine auctions. The auctions date back to the late 1700s and have been held almost continuously ever since. Over the years, the Hospices received and purchased many quality vineyards. The wines they produce are sold at auction in casks of 228 liters (about 300 bottles), on the third Sunday of November. The buyer must use traditional Burgundy bottles with labels issued by the Hospices. The labels include the appellation, the "*cuvée*" (name of the benefactor: Appendix A), the vintage year, and the name and address of the buyer. In 2003, 560 wine casks and 13 liquor casks were sold, at prices ranging from 1,700 Euros for the red Pernand-Vergelesses cuvée *Rameau-Lamarosse* to 40,000 Euros for the white Batard-Montrachet cuvée *Dames de Flandres*. The proceeds of the sale go to the hospital and are invested to fund its work.

The 1795 wine auction included 8 barrels. The 2005 auction involved 789 casks: 649 red and 140 white wines. The festive period surrounding the auction includes the annual meeting of the Chevaliers de Tastevin, a wine brotherhood created in 1934 and headquartered in the famous Clos De Vougeot.

---

2. See T. Echikson, *Noble Rot*. Norton, New York, 2004), and E. McCoy, *The Emperor of Wine: the Rise of Robert M. Parker, Jr. and the Rein of American Taste* (Harper Collins, New York, 2005).

3. See R.M. Parker Jr., *Bordeaux: A Consumer's Guide to the World's Finest Wines* (Simon and Schuster, New York, 1985), *Wine of the Rhone Valley* (Simon and Schuster, New York, 1997), and *Burgundy* (Simon and Schuster, New York, 1990).

4. D. Darlington, *The Chemistry of a 90+ wine* (The New York Times Magazine, August 7, 2005).

Figure 84: The main courtyard in the Hospices de Beaune (photo SKE).

Figures 85-86: Cover pages of the 1795 (left) and 2005 (right) auctions (courtesy: Musée de l'Hôtel-Dieu, Hospices de Beaune).

Burgundy produces numerous distinguished red (Pinot Noir) and white (Chardonnay) wines besides those of the Hospices. The quality increases with the specificity of the geographical name: region (e.g. *Bourgogne*), sub-region (e.g. *Côtes de Nuits*), village (e.g. *Beaune*), village-vineyard, "Premier Cru" wines (e.g. *Volnay-Santenots*), or simply vineyard, the highest rank, which are "Grand Cru" wines (e.g. *Richebourg*).

Beaujolais, south of Burgundy proper, is technically a part of it. It is the kingdom of the Gamay cultivar. The best wines are ranked with the "village" appellation, but even they should be drunk rather young, a few years at most. Unfortunately, most of the Beaujolais wine is released as "Beaujolais Primeur," a few weeks after the harvest. The wine has undergone the alcoholic but not the malolactic fermentation. In the early days, this wine was drunk in the region, right from the barrel. Today, it is marketed world-wide. Vast, some would say excessive, amounts of low-quality *Beaujolais Primeur* are bottled and shipped. This Primeur hurts the reputation of the high-quality Beaujolais wines.

The region of Chablis, north of Burgundy, produces memorable bone-dry Chardonnays, many of which age beautifully. Since the end of World War II, the malolactic fermentation is voluntarily induced in the spring, and the cellars are kept relatively warm for this reason. There are seven Grand Cru (Appendix D) and forty Premier Cru wines in Chablis.

Champagne

Champagne is further north. A lot has been said about winemaking in Champagne in earlier sections. These wines are secret blends of wines from different cultivars, regions, and vineyards within Champagne. A few of the wines are made exclusively from white (Chardonnay, listed "Blanc de Blanc") or red (Pinot Noir, listed "Blanc de Noir") grapes. But most champagne wines are blends of Chardonnay and Pinot Noir. The vintage year is normally not given. Instead, wines from different vintage years are mixed together in order to achieve a uniform taste and quality, characteristic of a given House. The word "brut," sometimes "extra brut," means that the wine is bone-dry. Other qualifications, such as "demi-sec," indicate that some sugar (sweet liquor) has been added. The switch from relatively sweet Champagnes to the very dry "brut" begins in the 1850s at the Champagne house of Perrier-Jouët. Today, it is the preferred Champagne style in France.

The best Champagne is vintaged. It is at most 10 to 15% of the production in the best (sunniest) growing seasons. The grapes must have been harvested in the marked vintage year. The "Cuvée" Champagnes, such as Cuvée Dom Pérignon, are normally vintaged. Pink Champagne is actually white Champagne to which some small volume of red wine, a Pinot Noir from the region, is added. A number of joint ventures between French Champagne houses and California are now firmly established, and the quality of the resulting Californian "champagnes" is high.

Alsace

The region of Alsace, on the German border, benefits from a dry climate, a hilly terrain, and a varied geology: granite, limestone, gneiss, schist and sandstone. In contrast to all other French AOC regions, the Alsatians often label their wines by the cultivar: Sylvaner, Pinot Blanc, Riesling, Pinot Noir, Gewurztraminer, Muscat d'Alsace, and Pinot Gris. The latter has been labeled "Tokay," but has nothing to do with the Hungarian Tokaji wine. For this reason, the "Tokay" label is no longer used in Alsace. The best vineyards of Alsace produce "Grand Cru" wines (Appendix D). The Alsatian appellations are still evolving.

The best Alsatian wines are dry and powerful: 13.5% alcohol is common. This contrasts with the sweeter wines produced across the border in Germany, for which 8.5 to 11% is more typical. The best German wines are delicate but few of them age as well as their Alsatian counterparts.

Figure 87: The Altenberg vineyard, a property of Frédéric Mochel in Bergbieten, produces Grand Cru Riesling, Muscat, and Gewurztraminer (photo SKE, and many thanks to Mother Nature for the rainbow).

Côtes du Rhône

The Côtes du Rhône wine region is divided into north (between the cities of Vienne and Valence) and south (north of Avignon) regions. Some twenty cultivars are allowed, among which the wonderful Syrah, Grenache, Viognier, Marsanne and Roussanne. One of the most famous wines is the Hermitage,[5] or Ermitage, a hill probably first planted by the Greeks. According to Thomas Jefferson, the white Hermitage is "the best wine in the world without any exception." Condrieu (Viognier cultivar) is another very big name. Gigondas, where the Grenache cultivar dominates, is one of the oldest regions. The name Gigondas comes from the Latin *jacunditas*, the village of happiness: it served as a resting place for deserving Roman soldiers.

Jura

The Jura region is most famous for its *vin jaune* (yellow wine). Most of the vineyards are planted with the Savagnin cultivar, and the rest with the Trousseau and the Poulsard. The Savagnin is hard to grow and its yield is very low, maybe 370 gallons per acre. The vin jaune is sold in a special bottle, the *clavelin*, with a capacity of 0.62 liters, vs. 0.75 for a conventional bottle. The reason for the unusual capacity of the clavelin is that one liter of fresh must produces 0.62 liters of vin jaune at the end of the process.

---

5. Note that the wines labeled Crozes-Hermitage come from a much larger region. Some of them are very good, but they are not the true Hermitage.

A special strain[6] of the yeast *saccharomyces cerevisiae* develops in the Jura on the Savagnin cultivar. It is called *torulaspora delbrueckii*. The same strain is found in Jerez, the sherry wine region of Southern Spain. The unusual flavor of the vin jaune, reminiscent of the fino sherry, is caused by this yeast. At the end of the fermentation, a thick whitish layer of yeast develops at the top of a cask of vin jaune. The same *flor* develops on top of a cask of sherry fino. The vin jaune must be kept at least 6 years and 3 months, undisturbed (no wine is removed or added). Once bottled, this wine is virtually indestructible.

The four geographical appellations in the Jura are *Arbois*, the oldest, *L'Etoile*, *Côtes du Jura*, and the famous *Château Chalon*. The best time to visit the region is the second Sunday of February, for the vin jaune festival. You may want to take a sweater and an umbrella, just in case.

Figure 88: A clavelin of Château Chalon (courtesy: Comité Interprofessionnel des vins du Jura, photo SKE).

As shown on the map, there are many other wine regions in France, and some of the wines they produce are excellent. Anjou produces mostly whites and rosés, the Loire has many well-known white wines (Pouilly-Fumé, Vouvray, Muscadet), Cahors is famous for its "black" wines, Corbières for its caves, and the list goes on.

ITALY

Hard work and government supervision in the decades following World War II increase the stature of Italian wines, some of which now rank with the best in the world. In the Wine Law of 1963, the Italian government introduces an appellation system similar to the French one, the *Denominazione di Origine Controllata* (DOC) and DOCG. The "G" stands for *e Garantia*, and primarily involves lower crop yields. The law regulates which cultivars can be used and many details of the viticulture, wine-making, aging, bottling, and labeling. The first DOC is awarded in 1966 to the Vernaccia di San Gimignano and the first DOCG in 1980 to a Brunello di Montalcino. Following revisions and expansions the law in 1980 and 1992, there are now four appellations in Italy. *Vino di Tavola* (table wines), *Indi-*

---

6. M. Kramer, *Making Sense of Wine* (Running Press, Philadelphia, 2003).

cazione Geografica Tipica (IGT), an intermediate category similar to the French VDQS, and the DOC and DOCG appellations, now expanded to include wines from non-native cultivars, in particular the so-called "super-Toscan" wines which contain Cabernet Sauvignon, imported from France. The recent appellation *Vigna* recognizes particularly superior wines from specific vineyards within a DOCG area. The "Classico" label on some Chianti bottles means that the grapes come from the production region originally delimited by the Duke of Tuscany in 1716. "Riserva" means that a wine has aged three or four years longer in wood barrels than other wines.

Figures 89-90: Main wine regions of Italy (maps: Kristin Reid).

Some Italian cultivars are well known and grow successfully in California, South America and elsewhere, for example the Sangiovese, Nebbiolo, Dolcetto, or Barbera. Many other delightful noble cultivars[7] are very typically Italian: Ruche, Frezia, Grignolino, Vermentino, Fiano just to name a few.

Italian wine regions cover the entire country. In the north, *Valle d'Aosta*, the smallest Italian wine region, produces wines from French cultivars such as the Chardonnay and the Pinot Noir. In *Trentino-Alto Adige*, one finds Pinot Noir and Cabernet Sauvignon, as well as the indigenous Lagrein and Schiava. The *Piedmont* is famous for the powerful Barolo and Barbaresco wines, both made from the superlative Nebbiolo grape. Close seconds are the Barbera and Dolcetto. For happy hour, I recommend a fresh Moscato d'Asti, although the Italians drink this fruity and delightfully sparkling wine for dessert.

Lombardy is famous for its sparkling wines; *Veneto* for the Valpolicella, the (dry) sparkling Prosecco, and the powerful Amarone. *Friuli-Venezia Giulia* is best known for its dry white wines (e.g., Pinot Grigio) but local cultivars are also used such as the Ribella, Refosco, or Tocai Friulino. Modern experiments in ancient technology are also taking place. A winemaker from the Friuli, Josko Gravner, ferments and ages his wines in huge terra-cotta amphorae lined with beeswax, buried in the ground. This technique is reminiscent of the Roman dolia

---

7. P. Dallas, *Italian Wines* (Faber and Faber, London, 1989); B. Anderson, *The Wines of Italy* (Simon and Schuster, New York, 1992).

and involves neither stainless steel nor wooden barrels. Dry white wines from the Pigato and Vermentino grapes are typical of *Ligura*, the coastal region around Genova. *Emilia-Romagna* is home to the Lambrusco, a light sparkling red wine. *Tuscany*, with Florence at its center, is best known for the Chianti. The main grape is the Sangiovese. The famous Brunello di Montalcino and the Vino Nobile di Montepulciano are typical Tuscans as well.

Figure 91: One example of little-known and delicious wine from the Piedmont, made from the (white) Timorasso cultivar (courtesy: Claudio Mariotto in Vho, southern Piedmont).

The wine production in Central and Southern Italy is mostly local. Their names and examples of local cultivar are *Umbria* (Sagrantino di Montefalco), *Marche* (Verdicchio), *Latium* around Rome (Malvasia, Trebbiano), *Abruzzi* and *Molise* (Montepulciano), *Campania* around Naples (Aglianico), *Apulia* (Primitivo), *Basilicata* (Aglianico del Vulture), *and Calabria* (Greco). *Sardinia* produces interesting wines from the Vermentino (white) and Monica (red) grapes. *Sicily*, often associated with strong but otherwise common wines, is now producing very interesting and high quality wines from local cultivars (Nero d'Avola, Nerello Mascalese, Zibibbo) as well as from newcomers to the region, such as the Chardonnay. The list continues. Italy has many fascinating wines. Trips to Italy are very enjoyable indeed!

SPAIN

The Spanish "DO" system, first established in 1933, is broadly similar to the French AOC. New appellations proliferate in the 1960s, but investment in technological infrastructure remains insufficient for a long time. The wines from Sherry are known since centuries, and the region of Rioja[8] has some notoriety as well. Following World War II, the overall reputation of most Spanish wines is low. The dictatorship of Generalissio Franco discourages free enterprise and

---

8. The Marqués de Riscal and Marqués de Murrieta (Ygay) estates, the oldest in the region, are established in the late 1850s.

foreign investment. Neither the quality nor the reputation of Spanish wines increases under Franco.

On November 20, 1975, Franco dies. In Barcelona and other cities, the police confiscate all the champagne they can find in wine stores, restaurants, and bars in a futile attempt to prevent people from celebrating. The Catalans celebrate anyway. On November 22, Prince Juan Carlos is proclaimed King of Spain, albeit with limited powers within the new multi-party democracy. Spain is breathing again. The wine industry begins a steady climb.

The Spanish wine laws are updated several times, especially after Spain joins the European Union. The most recent update, the Vineyard and Wine Act, dates back to 2003. The wines are classified according to quality regulations imposed in specific regions as well as to aging characteristics. The highest geographical appellation, *Vinos de Pago* (estate wines), includes wines from specific vineyards of recognized prestige. The *Vinos de Denominación de Origen Calificada* (DOCa, qualified denomination of origin) is for wines that have achieved high levels of recognition for extended periods of time — that means DO status for at least ten years. The wines are strictly regulated and bottled in the region of origin. The *Vinos de Denominación de Origen* (DO, wines with an appellation of origin), is similar to the French AOC appellation. Finally, there are *Vinos de Calidad con Indicacion Geografica*, and *Vinos de la Tierra*, which are roughly equivalent to the French VDQS and Vin de Pays appellations. The table wines are the most common and least regulated.

In addition to the appellations of origin listed above, the aging characteristics of wines are also regulated. All the wines can be labeled *Vino noble*, *Vino añejo*, or *Vino Viejo*, which mean that the wine has aged a minimum of 18, 24, or 36 months, respectively. The aging can be done in 600-liter barrels and/or bottles. Still (non-sparkling) wines can also be labeled *Crianza*, *Reserva*, or *Gran Reserva* if they are aged in 330-liters oak casks and then in bottles for a total of 24, 36, or 60 months, respectively. The minimum time in casks is 6 months for *Crianza*, 12 for *Reserva*, and 18 for *Gran Reserva*.

Figures 92-93: Main wine regions of Spain (maps Kristin Reid).

The increasingly strict regulations imposed by the government create a reward system for producing quality rather than relying on market forces. The quality of the best Spanish wines has now reached spectacular levels. Today, Spain produces many world-class wines.[9] The *Vega Sicilia* from the fabulous Ribera del Duero region is among the most famous ones.

In addition to Rioja and Ribera del Duero, other wine districts produce high-quality and distinct wines such as Priorato or Penedés. The traditional Spanish red wines are macerated with stems in open vats, and then aged in large, old, wooden barrels. Recent developments include the systematic use of stainless steel tanks for fermentation, and new French oak barrels for aging.

Typical white Spanish cultivars include the Albariño,[10] Treixadura, Verdejo, Viura and Airén. Imported grapes such as the Chardonnay and Sauvignon Blanc are allowed in several regions. For red wines, the Tempranillo (a.k.a. Tinto Fino) is the best known cultivar. It is sometimes referred to as the Spanish Cabernet, even though it is rounder and softer. Other exciting red grapes include the Garnacha, Monastrel, and Tinto de Toro. The imported Cabernet Sauvignon and Merlot are often used in blends.

Figure 94: The intense Vega Sicilia (courtesy: Grupo Peñín, Madrid).

The Sherry is produced in the chalky soils region around the city of Jerez de la Frontera. The dominant cultivar is the very dry and acidic Palomino Bianco, but the much sweeter Pedro Ximénez ("PX" on the label) and Moscatel grow on a few percent of the planted area. Sherry begins as a dry white wine with about 11% alcohol, fortified with grape alcohol to about 15% to produce the Fino (in Jerez), Manzanilla (in Sanlúcar), Amontillado or Palo Cortado sherries. This moderate fortification allows the yeast to develop a thick "flor" on the surface of the wine in the cask. The flor protects the wine from oxygen and imparts a characteristic flavor to the wine. In order to produce an Oloroso sherry, the wine is fortified to 18%, which does prevent a flor from developing.

The sherry is aged in a solera. The system consists of four (sometimes three) layers of casks in which the wine ages. The bottom casks are the *solera*. They contain the oldest sherry. The upper layers of casks are the first, second,

---

9. K. McWhirter and C. Metcalfe, *Encyclopedia of Spanish and Portuguese Wines* (Fireside, Simon and Schuster, New York, 1991).

10. *Albariño* refers to a "white [grape] from the Rhine."

and third *criaderas*. At most one-third of each cask in the solera is used when bottling sherry. These casks are then filled with sherry from the casks in the first criadera, which themselves are topped off with wine from the second criadera, etc. The top criadera is filled with the new sherry. Thus, in each layer, the freshness and energy of a younger wine blends in with the softness and maturity of an older wine. The date on a solera sherry refers to the year when a particular solera was started. Some soleras are well over a century old.

Figure 95: A solera in the Sherry region (courtesy of the Spanish Institute for Foreign Trade, ICEX, photo Carlos Tejero).

PORTUGAL

Portugal has a rich wine history and today produces many excellent table wines[11] in addition to the fortified Ports and Madeiras. Some of these wines are deep, powerful, and long-aging reds, others are delicate whites and others still are light and crisp such as the *vinho verde*. Many of noble cultivars are typically Portuguese, such as the exquisite Touriga Nacional, the softer Castelão, or the powerful Alfracheiro.

The Ports are the most regulated and controlled wines in the world. However, regarding table wines, the Portuguese wine laws are not yet as advanced as they are in France, Italy or Spain. The highest-quality wines belong to the *Denominação de Origem Controlada* (DOC, controlled denomination of origin) appellation. The rules governing the cultivar, viticulture, and wine-making are comparable to those of the French AOC system. There are now 14 DOC regions

---

11. Jan Read, *The Wines of Portugal* (Faber and Faber, London, 1987); See also *Vinhos e Aguardentes de Portugal* (Instituto de Vinha e do Vinho, Lisboa, updated periodically).

in Portugal. Some of them are well-known (Dão, Douro, Madeira) but many wine drinkers are still unfamiliar with others (Langos, Protiamo, Travora). Many wines of recognized quality, albeit of inferior quality to DOC wines, belong to the *Indicação de Proveniencia Regulamentada* (IPR) appellation, which is about equivalent to the French VDQS.

Figures 96-97: The main wine regions of Portugal (maps Kristin Reid).

In recent years, some of the best vineyards in the Douro have been used to produce dry table wines rather than Port. These are among the very best in Portugal. Other wine regions north east and north of Lisbon (Estremadura and Ribatejo) and in the south of the country (Alentejo) have modernized since Portugal joined the European Union in 1986, and their wines could be the next hot thing.

In the old days, red wines were pressed in open stone vats (*lagares*), fermented with stalks and aged for years in old barrels. Few wines are now made this way. Since the late 1980s, de-stemming, pneumatic presses, stainless steel vats, dried yeast and other technological advances are common.

Port wines come from demarcated regions in the upper Douro River. "Douro" is a contraction of *Rio do Ouro*, "river of gold." The terraced vineyards, on spectacular steep and rocky hills, stretch for some 70 miles up to the Spanish border. The most important of the 30 or so cultivars in the region are the Touriga Nacional, Touriga Francesca, Tinta Roriz,[12] Tinta Barocca, and the fine and delicate Tinto Cão. Early in the fall, the grapes are harvested, pressed, and the juice macerated. When the alcohol concentration reaches about 6%, the must is run off into casks containing *aguardente*, a grape brandy at 77%. The aguardente-to-must ratio is 1:4. The alcohol kills the yeast, which stops the fermentation and preserves natural sugar: A typical port has 20% alcohol and 10% residual sugar. The trick is to extract as much color and tannin as possible in a short period of

---

12. It is called "Tempranillo" in Spain.

time, thus leaving enough residual sugar in the wine. The best way to achieve this is foot-treading, which is still done for the best ports.

Figure 98: In the beginning of the foot-treading process, a row of workers walk back and forth across the stone vat to crush the berries. After a couple of hours, the fermentation picks up and it is time for music as the workers dance in the vat. The entire process lasts about 12 hours (courtesy: Niepoort VINHOS, photo Manfred Klimek).

In the spring following the harvest, the new wine is transported to Vila Nova de Gaia, on the south bank of the Douro, across from the city of Porto.[13] It spends two years in wooden casks, and then its fate is decided. The two broad categories of red ports are *Tawny* — mahogany color, soft, delicate — and *Ruby* — brilliant red, more intense and powerful. The latter never spends more than 6 years in wood. Starting with the best, the categories are as follows.

Tawny Ports: *Colheita,* which means "harvest" or "crop," is a tawny from a single vintage, aged at least 7 years in wood, often much longer. The port houses best known for Colheita ports are Kopke, Niepoort, Cálem, and Burmeister. *Aged tawnies* are blends of many (dozens) wines. The label shows the average age of the blend: "10," "20," "30," or "over 40" years. Wood-aging, with periodic racking and blending, allows more contact with air than bottle-aging, which softens the wine. Then there are many common tawnies. Their quality varies. The best ones are aged over seven years in wood, the cheapest ones are blended with white port to produce the tawny color.

---

13. Until 1987, it was illegal to age, bottle, and ship port from anywhere but Vila Nova de Gaia. The goal was to prevent the wine from suffering from the "Douro burn," caused by the high summer temperatures in the Upper Douro. Today, air-conditioning makes it possible to prevent the burn and several Port Houses are headquartered in the Upper Douro valley, such as Quinta do Infantado and Quinta do Crasto.

Figure 99: Vintage ports from the early 1900s, behind bars at San-deman in Vila Nova de Gaia (photo SKE)

Ruby Ports: *Vintage* requires a "declaration of vintage" by the Instituto do Vinho do Porto. Shippers request such a decla-ration only in the best vintage years, and then only 1 to 2% of the best port becomes Vintage. The wine is bottled between its 2nd and 3rd year and ages in bottles. Many believe that Taylor-Fladgate produces the best vintage ports. The *Single-Quinta Vintage* is a ruby port from a spe-cific vintage and estate such as e.g., Dow's *Quinta do Bomfim* or Warre's *Quinta da Cavadinha*. The wine spends 2–4 years in wood and ages in bottles. *Vintage Char-acter* port is a blend of several vintage years but bottled late, often just as the tawny color begins to show. *Late-Bottled Vintage* (LBV) is from a single vintage and spends 4–6 years in wood. Most LBVs are filtered and bottled ready to drink. Some of them lack distinction. The best ones, labeled "traditional," are not filtered and con-tinue to age in bottles. There are many common rubies. Their quality varies.

The rare *Garrafeira* is a port from a single vintage, aged 2 years in wood then many years in 5- or 10-liter glass demijohns. It has deep fruit and color, but is soft and silky. Niepoort is one of the few port houses producing this remarkable port.

Germany

Germany[14] has 13 wine regions, some of which have sub-regions: Ahr, Mit-telrhein, Mosel-Saar-Ruwer, Nahe, Rheingau, Rheinhessen, Rheinpfaltz, Hes-

---

14. I. Jamieson, *German Wines* (Faber and Faber, London, 1991).

sische-Bergstrasse, Franken, Württemberg, and Baden are in the former "West" Germany, roughly along the river Rhein. While the nearby Alsatian wines tend to have little or no residual sugar and emphasize strength, the German wines tend to have some, or a lot, of sweetness. In former "East" Germany, the wine regions are Saale-Unstrut and Sachsen.

The most abundant cultivars are the Riesling, Pinot Blanc (*Weissburgunder*), Pinot Noir (*Spätburgunder*), Silvaner, and Müller-Thurgau. Smaller areas are planted with Gewürztraminer, and purely German cultivars such as the Gutedel or Kerner.

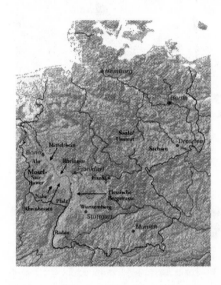

Figures 100-101: Wine regions of Germany (maps: Kristin Reid).

The quality of a German wine is often linked to the degree of ripeness of the berries at harvest time, that is to their sugar (and therefore alcohol) content. "QbA" stands for *Qualitäswein bestimmter Anbaugebiete* and "QmP" for *Qualitäswein mit Prädikat*. The QbA wines have low alcohol content (5.9-9.4%). The QmP category includes the best German wines. In order of increased sugar and alcohol content, and also price, are the *Kabinett*, *Spätlase* (late harvest), *Auslese* and *Beerenauslese* (which refer to the selection of bunches for concentration or ripeness), *Eiswein* (harvest delayed until the first freeze) and *Trockenbeerensaulese*. The latter wines often involve some degree of noble rot and may exceed 20% alcohol.

The German wine laws, especially those of 1971 and 1994, seem to encourage the blending of wines from the best vineyards with lesser wines. This results from a strange idea. Instead of recognizing and protecting a particularly good vineyard, the German laws extend regions within a given appellation, thus increasing the volume produced at the expense of quality. For example, in the early 1900s, the *Wehlener Sonnenuhr* wine[15] came only from a 25 acre region. The appellation was extended to 86 acres in 1953, then 143 acres, and is now about

---

15. I. Jamieson, *German Wines* (Faber and Faber, London, 1991).

116. As a result, a prestigious name on the label does not guarantee that the wine in the bottle actually comes from the vineyard the label refers to. It is best to know the producer and/or the wine merchant. The indication *Einzellagen* ("estate-bottled" is an approximate translation) provides some reassurance.

OTHER WESTERN EUROPEAN COUNTRIES

In addition to France, Italy, Spain, Portugal, and Germany which are among the top dozen wine producers in the world, several other Western European countries also produce wines and deserve to be mentioned. The largest ones are Greece, Austria, and Switzerland, but wines are also made elsewhere. Cyprus produces powerful dessert wines and southern England dry white wines. Ice wines are made as far north as Sweden. Most of these wines are consumed locally and are difficult to find far from the production region.

Greece

While the tourist-oriented Retsina is probably the most recognizable Greek wine, many other wines are produced in Greece,[16] and some of them are excellent. The Naoussa Gran Reserva for example, made from the local Xynomavro cultivar, ages very nicely.

Austria

Today, Austria has four wine regions: Weinland Osterreich is by far the largest with almost 92% of the vineyards, Steirerland (less than 7%), Wien (just over 1%), and Bergland which covers the western half of the country but has only 0.04% of Austria's vineyards. The regions are subdivided into 19 wine areas. The country produces more white than red wines, with over 20 white and a dozen red cultivars.

Switzerland

For many years, Switzerland was best known for the crisp, light white wine from the Chasselas cultivar which dominated the landscape. Today, wines from over 30 cultivars are produced. Small vineyards are experimenting with ancient, forgotten cultivars: Rèze, Païen, Lafnetscha, Eyholzer Roter, Completer, Räuschling — here too, there is a lot to be discovered.

---

16. N. Manessis, *The Illustrated Greek Wine Book* (Olive Press, Corfu, 2000).

EASTERN EUROPE

Viticulture exists in south-eastern Europe since Greek or Roman times, well-documented in Tracia, for example, at the time of the Gaeto-Dacian king Burebista. There is every reason to believe that wine has long been produced in most of what today are Bulgaria, Croatia, the Czech Republic, Hungary, Lithuania, Macedonia, Romania, Russia, Slovakia, Slovenia, and Ukraine. With the integration of Eastern Europe into the European Union, these wines are faced with the challenge of penetrating Western markets and becoming known for their own unique characteristics.

Hungary

A few Eastern European wines have made a name for themselves. One is the Hungarian *Tokaji Aszú*. *(Tokaj*, the city, and *Tokaji* or *Tokay*, the wine or region, have nothing to do with the Alsatian "tokay," which is another name for the Pinot Gris.) Tokaji Aszú involves noble-rot wine from the *Furmint, Hárslevelü, Muscat Lunel*, and *Orémus* cultivars, grown on volcanic hills in the *Tokaj-Hegyalja* wine region of Hungary. The word "Aszú" refers to the dry noble-rot grapes. Tokaji Aszú wines have a unique and long-lasting flavor, quite distinct from that of other noble-rot wines (Sauternes or Beerenauslese). Most Tokaji Aszú wines are labeled by *puttonyos*. A putton is a bucket containing about 25 kg of Aszú grains. A Tokaji Aszú labeled 3 to 6 puttonyos is one in which 3 to 6 buckets of Aszú grains have been mixed into 136 liters of dry Tokaji wine.[17]

 The rarest of all, the *Tokaji Eszencia* (or *Esszencia*) is made from the drops that slowly ooze from the pile of Aszú grains under their own weight.[18] About four tons of Aszú grains are needed to produce one liter of Eszencia, and the

Figures 104-105: Aszú grains (above) and one putton (courtesy: Alain Gourdis, Chateau Pajzos)

---

17. The Aszú grains affect the amount of residual sugar in the wine: three puttonyos (the minimum) result in over 60 grams per liter; four = over 90; five = over 120; and six = 150+. Tokaji Aszú Eszencia has 8 - 9 puttonyos: over 180 g/l. The high acidity of dry wine involved in the blend is critical.

process takes a couple of months. The sugar content is so high (over 250 g/l) that the fermentation may take years. With an alcohol concentration of just 4% it is less in demand in today's market.

Romania

Viticulture is ancient in Romania, and its wines have been praised since Roman times. In the late 19th century, phylloxera strikes with a vengeance and most of the old cultivars are replaced by French cultivars grafted onto American rootstock; a few original cultivars such as Zghihara de Huşi, Crâmposia de Dragaşani, Feteasca Neagrâ or Tâmâioasa remain, but most of the vineyards grow the much more familiar cabernet sauvignon, merlot, pinot noir, chardonnay, etc. There are numerous wine regions in the country, but the four most important ones are Tarnave, Dealu Mare, Murfatlar, and Cotnari.

Tarnave is in Transylvania, a high plateau in central Romania, surrounded by the Carpathian Mountains. Mostly white wines are produced. Dealu Mare is on the southern slopes of the Carpathian Mountains. The climate is much softer. The region produces mostly red wines with French cultivars. Murfatlar is very close to the Black Sea. The region is warm, sunny, and humid in the fall. The production includes rich red wines as well as dessert wines, often involving some degree of noble rot.

The most famous and distinctive Romanian wine region is Cotnari. It is located in north-east of the country, on the eastern hills of the mountains. The native Grasa, Tâmâioasa, Frâncuşa, and Feteasca Alba cultivars develop the noble rot and are used to produce luscious dessert wines, often compared the to Hungarian Tokaji Aszú. In his monumental trilogy *USA*, Dos Pasos describes Cotnari as a fashionable drink in New York in the 1920s.

The Czech Republic

Viticulture in the south of Moravia, the south-eastern region of the Czech Republic where over 90% its wines are produced today, exists since Roman times. However, it is in the late Middle Ages that the first decrees regulating wines and viticulture are issued by Charles IV (1342-1378). Modern wine laws are established in 1995. They specify the geographical appellations; specify the quality controls and the classification.

The recognized geographical areas are the region (oblast), sub-region (podoblast), village (obec) and vineyard (tra). A wide range of cultivars are found in the Czech Republic, some of which are local (Svatovavrinecké or Muškát Moravský) and others imported, possibly during the replanting that follows the phylloxera infestation (such as the Cabernet Sauvignon or Gewurtztraminer.

---

18. The Romans used a similar technique to produce their best and most expensive wines.

United States

In 1855, the Swiss/French botanist Alphonse de Candolle[19] (1806-1893) publishes the first serious study of viticultural climates based on climatic data, which were then becoming available. He notices that vines start active growth in the spring when air temperatures exceed 50^F, and proposes a "degree-days" criterion to characterize the suitability of specific regions for viticulture. His ideas are systematically applied in California in 1944 by the UC Davis Professors Amerine and Winkler.[20] They defined five viticultural regions based on the number of *degrees* above 50^F times the number of *days* above 50^F, over the seven months growing season (April through October). Region I has fewer than 2,500 degree-days, and is the best region to produce dry table wines. It includes the Carneros district and Santa Cruz. For each of regions II through IV, 500 degree-days are added. Most of Napa and Sonoma Valleys are Region II. Region V has over 4,000 degree-days, is suited to the production of table or drying grapes. It includes the dry and hot Central Valley of California.

The Amerine-Winkler viticultural regions serve as a guide for replanting California with noble cultivars following Prohibition and World War II. This involves substantial and long-term investment, and the US wine industry slowly recovers. The first boost occurs in the early 1950s with waves of post-World War II European immigrants. This is the period when *refrigerated* stainless steel tanks[21] with rotary compressors appear. Three materials are now involved in winemaking: stainless steel for temperature-controlled fermentation, wood for maturation and the addition of tannins, and then glass bottles for aging.

Until the 1960s, much of the US wine production consists of low quality sweet and/or fortified wines. Cultivar labeling is introduced by Frank Schoomaker in the 1960s. In 1966, Robert Mondavi bottles his first Cabernet Sauvignon. In 1968, the production of dry table wines labeled "Bourgogne" (for reds) or "Chablis" (for whites) overtakes that of fortified wines. However, such labels provide little useful information about the content of the bottle, as winemakers simply borrow French appellations and use them as a way to advertise the wine, without much regard for ethics. Until the 1970s the reputation of US wines in general is poor. No European restaurant has American wines on its wine list. In this period only a few dedicated winemakers in Napa and Sonoma valleys produce quality wines.

---

19. Alphonse de Candolle is the son of another famous botaniste, Augustin Pyrame de Candolle (1779-1841).
20. M.A. Amerine and A.J. Winkler, Hilgardia **15**, 493(1944).
21. In Wine Review **3**, 15 (1935), O.M. Shelton notes that Cameo Vineyards already owns four stainless steel tanks in 1935.

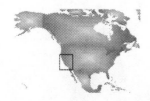

Figures 106-107: Main wine regions of California (maps: Kristin Reid).

In May 1976, the Englishman Stephen Spurrier, co-founder of L'Académie du Vin, organizes a blind tasting at the Hotel Intercontinental in Paris.[22] There are eleven judges: Stephen Spurrier and his assistant Patricia Gallagher, and nine highly respected French judgessuch as Pierre Bréjoux — inspector general of the Appellation d'Origine Contrôlée board, Odette Kahn — editor of the Revue de Vin de France, Christian Vannequé — head sommelier of the three-star Tour d'Argent restaurant, and Aubert de Villaine from the Domaine de la Romanée-Conti. The tasting includes ten Cabernet Sauvignon wines, four from Bordeaux and six from California, and ten Chardonnay wines, again four from Burgundy and six from California.

To everyone's surprise, the 1973 Stag's Leap Cabernet Sauvignon from Napa Valley ranks first among the reds with a mean rating of 14.14. It defeats the French 1970 Château Mouton Rothschild with a mean rating of 14.09, a statistically irrelevant difference but startling nonetheless. Next are the 1970 Château Montrose (13.64), 1970 Château Haut-Brion (13.23), 1971 Ridge Montebello (12.14), 1971 Château Leoville-Las-Case (11.18), 1970 Heitz Martha's Vineyars (10.36), 1972 Clos du Val (10.14), 1971 Mayacamas (9.77), and 1969 Freemark Abbey (9.64). Among the whites, the 1973 Château Montelena (Napa Valley) beats a French 1973 Meursault-Charmes, followed by the 1974 Chalone Vineyards and 1973 Spring Mountain from California, and the French 1973 Beaune Clos des Mouches. Next are the 1972 Freemark Abbey, 1973 Batard-Montrachet, 1972 Puligny-Montrachet Les Pucelles, 1972 Veedercrest, and 1973 David Bruce from Santa Cruz Mountains. Although two wines from California win the event, the French wines are ranked higher on average.

---

22. G.M. Taber, Judgment of Paris: California versus France and the Wine Tasting that Changed the World (Simon and Schuster, New York, 2005).

Figures 108-109: At the 1976 Paris wine tasting. Left: the judges at work. Right: Patricia Gallagher (left), Stephen Spurrier (middle), and Odette Kahn, one of the French judges (right) (photos: Bella Spurrier).

Figures 110-111: The winners in Paris (courtesy: Stag's Leap Wine Cellars, left, and Chateau Montelena, right).

Since the Middle Ages until that day, French wines were, by definition, the best in the world. All the other wines were judged relative to them. New styles of wines and blends that could not be compared to French wines were discouraged. Suddenly, the world realizes that American wines not only compete with the best French wines, but may win as judged by French judges. This change of attitude toward non-French wines is the real legacy of the 1976 Paris wine tasting.

A burst of investment sweeps through California and the rest of the US. New vineyards are planted in Illinois, Georgia, Maryland, Texas (near Lubbock in West Texas and the Hill Country in Central Texas), Washington, and Oregon. Abandoned vineyards are restarted in Virginia, Ohio and New York. Researchers at UC Davis design cultivars suited to particular climatic conditions and produce detailed maps showing which cultivars are most likely to perform best in each region. The vines are grafted on phylloxera-resistant rootstock. Different rootstocks offer varying degrees of protection and productivity. They have romantic names such as 161-49, 41B, 110 Richter, or AXR1. The latter, a *vinifera x rupestris* hybrid, is the most widely used during the boom of the 1970s. It is productive but not very resistant. Phylloxera has been feeding on it in recent years and a lot of replanting had to be done. Today, there are wineries in every state, including North Dakota and Alaska. Thomas Jefferson would be very happy indeed.

Government regulations in the United States are nowhere near as strict as in Western Europe. It is assumed that market forces as well as the skills, technical knowledge, and dedication of the winemaker suffice. The Bureau of Alcohol, Tobacco, and Firearms has limited powers to enact regulations through the Federal Alcohol Administration Act. The authority does not include setting quality standards, much less inspecting how vines are pruned or which cultivars are grown. The word "Controlled," prominent in European laws, is absent here. The law recognizes over 160 "American Viticultural Areas" (AVAs) and the wine produced in these areas can be recognized as such. The sizes of the AVAs vary from 26,000 square miles ("Ohio River Valley") to 0.25 square mile ("Cole Ranch"). The label "Estate Bottled" means that the grapes are grown, the wine made and bottled within the same AVA. Today, California produces some 90% of the US wine, with almost 1,400 wineries and 5,000 grape growers.

Canada

Canada has an appellation of origin system called Vintners Quality Alliance (VQA) which recognizes the origin of the grapes used to make the wine. The VQA system is implemented in Ontario since 1988 and British Columbia since 1990. Ontario has three "designated viticultural areas" (Niagara Peninsula, Pelee Island, Lake Erie North Shore) and British Columbia as four Okanagan Valley, Similkameen Valley, Fraser Valley, Vancouver Island).

Wine is made in southern Ontario, Canada, since the 19th century. But until the 1970s, this involves the American Concord and the Catawba. Then, imported v. vinifera cultivars, mainly Chardonnay, Riesling, Cabernet Franc, and Merlot, are planted and prosper in several regions where microclimates are favorable. In Ontario, these are the Niagara Peninsula and the Northern Shore of Lake Erie. In British Columbia, it is the dry Okanagan Valley. Canada is best-known for its icewines. This type of wine is accidentally discovered in Germany in the late 19th century, when an early deep freeze forces winemakers to crush frozen grapes. The ice and the water it contains stay behind, leaving a concentrated wine. The appropriate conditions for producing icewine, 18-20F for at least 24 hours before harvest, are often realized in Canada.

CENTRAL AND SOUTH AMERICA

The emergence of modern wines in Central and South America following World War II is delayed for a long time. Substantial investment is required to upgrade the technology, plant new vineyards with appropriate cultivars, and then sell the wines — which implies marketing and distribution channels in the United States and Europe. All of this implies foreign investment, which in turns implies political stability and free markets, in addition to the prospect of reasonable return on the investment. Thus, the turbulent political climate in many countries of Central and South America prevent the development of a competitive wine industry for decades, even in countries where the potential for viticulture is great, such as Chile or Argentina.

Argentina

At the end of World War II, Juan Perón becomes President. During the next decade, the country partially recovers from a depression that begun in the 1920s. Perón is forced out of office and leaves the country in 1955. A 20-years period of political instability ensues. In 1973, Perón return to power, but dies the following year. His wife Isabel becomes President, but she is overthrown in 1975. Another period of economic and political instability follows, with a succession of mostly incompetent military governments. All aspects of the economy are affected, including wines. By the late 1980s, most of Argentina's production consists of low-quality mass-produced wines. Wine in Argentina is "plentiful and cheap." Then, in 1989, Carlos Menem of the Peronist party is elected President. Free-market and other reforms slowly lead to political and economic stability, Menem remains President until 1999. The next few years are difficult again, but democracy is now well established in Argentina.

Following the election of Carlos Menem, foreign investment increases. For wines, this means upgraded equipment (stainless steel tanks, new oak barrels, etc.) as well as vineyards replanted with quality cultivars. Today, the dominant noble red cultivars are the Malbec, Cabernet Sauvignon, Merlot (from France), the Tempranillo (from Spain), and the Sangiovese, Nebbiolo, Barbera, Dolcetto, and Freisa (from Italy). In white, they are the Chardonnay from France and the Torrontes, from Spain. The largest and best wine region is Mendoza (Maipu). To the north, the second-largest wine region, San Juan, is much dryer and hotter. Further north is La Rioja, which produces mostly white wines. Several relatively recent wines regions even further north, Catamarca, Tucuman, Salta, and Jujuy as well as south of Mendoza down to Rio Negro benefit from excellent growing conditions and show promise.

Chile

The political situation in Chile is quite stable until the 1970s. The government of Salvador Allende nationalizes key industries and pushes social reforms. The result is high inflation, social unrest, and economic sanctions imposed by the US President, Richard Nixon. The opposition to Allende in Chile encourages a military coup in 1973, during which Salvador Allende dies. The commander of the army, Augusto Pinochet (1915-) takes power. The constitution is suspended and Congress dissolved. Pinochet stays in power until 1990. His dictatorship proves hazardous to life, liberty, the pursuit of happiness, and free enterprise. The domestic demand for wine drops under his rule and nearly half the vineyards are abandoned. In the late 1980s, the closed-doors policies are reversed. The Spaniard Miguel Torres brings modern wine technology to Chile.

Figures 112-113: Main wine regions of Chile and Argentina (maps: Kristin Reid).

Democracy returns in 1990 with the election of Patricio Aylwin. The implementation of free market policies leads to a rapid economic growth. This is particularly true for the wine industry. Indeed, Chile not only benefits from exceptionally good conditions for viticulture, including water from the Andes Mountains for irrigation, but also from the absence of mildew and phylloxera. Vine cuttings can be planted without expensive grafting on American rootstock. Numerous investors from California (such as Mondavi or Kendall-Jackson) and France (Eric de Rothschild for example) establish wineries. Some 25,000 new acres of noble cultivars are planted by 1993. The technology improves, and quality factors such as the use of small oak barrels implemented. The export of high-quality Chilean wines begins.

Government regulations impose maximum yields and a few rules. For example, the "75% rule" established in 1995 states that at least 75% of the content of a bottle must match the description on the label. A new appellation system regulates the varietals, vintage, and exact geographical origin. However, the rules for Reserva, Gran Reserva, and Reserva Especial labeling are vague. The wine regions extend from north of Santiago to the south in a series of valleys perpendicular to the Pacific: Aconcagua, Casablanca, Maipo, Rapel, Colchagua, Curico, and Maule valleys. The dominant cultivars in Chile are the Cabernet Sauvignon, Merlot, Chardonnay and Sauvignon Blanc.

Figure 114: A Chilean Cabernet Sauvignon made by the Alsatian Dominique Massenez (courtesy Los Boldos)

Brazil and Uruguay

At the end of World War over 90% of Brazil's production is located in the southernmost state, Rio Grande do Sol, and not much attention is paid to wine. Mostly hybrid grapes are grown, and the quality is unremarkable. In the 1960s, European cultivars are imported and the wines are advertised. Today, some 20 French, German, and Italian cultivars are used to produce an array of wines. A few of those wines can now be found on the international market. Uruguay, just south of Rio Grande do Sol, produces wines from half-a-dozen French cultivars. The most typical one in Uruguay is the Tannat, a grape used in France mostly for blends, as it adds color and tannin to weaker wines. In Uruguay however, a variety of characteristic wines is produced with this cultivar.

Mexico

The oldest wine-producing country in the Americas, Mexico is still a small producer. The best Mexican wines today are produced in the Valle de Guadalupe, Baja California, south of California-Mexico border. It begins in the 1930s in the Valley of Santo Tomas, when immigrants discover abandoned plants and equipment. In 1938, this becomes the Bodegas Santo Tomás. Today, eight wineries, all located within a 75-mile radius of San Diego, CA, produce interesting wines, some of which are exported. L.A. Cetto produces a memorable a Neb-biolo.

SOUTH AFRICA

For a variety of financial and political reasons, South African wines emerge internationally only in the mid-1970s. Many countries still boycott South Africa (and its wines) because of the racial Apartheid policies of the white government. The boycott lasts until February 1990, when president Frederik Willem de Klerk declares the end of Apartheid, He also states that he is in favor of a democratic South Africa. The African National Congress is officially recognized, and its president, Nelson Mandela, is released from Robben Island after 27 years behind bars. Mandela becomes the first black President of South Africa in 1994.

The Wine of Origin certification scheme is officially instituted in 1973, in accordance with the Wine, Other Fermented Beverages and Spirits Act of 1957. The smallest demarcated production unit is the Estate, which consists of one or more bordering farms, as long as it is farmed as a unit and has cellars on the estate where the wine is produced. There are over 50 recognized estates. The second-largest area of origin, the Ward, is used for a small demarcated viticultural area which includes farms. A ward is usually, but not necessarily, part of a District — the third largest area of origin. Jonkershoek Valley is in the Stellenbosch District, but Constantia is not part of any district. Next are 16 districts, such as Paarl or Stellenbosch. The fourth demarcated production unit is a Region, which is a combination of districts or portions of districts. An even more general appellation, defined since 1993, is the Geographical Unit. They are Western Cape and Northern Cape. A wine labeled as a Geographical Unit may not claim Wine of Origin status. Since 1980, it is easier for winegrowers to obtain import permits for improved vine cuttings.

The wine-producing area lies within 100 miles of Cape Town. Constantia, Stellenbosch and Paarl are wine regions of particular interest. The soil, growing conditions and know-how are excellent. Today, South Africa produces a number of world-class wines — as well as many common wines. Many of the top-quality South African wines benefit from aging.

The Constantia region is now divided into several estates which include Groot Constantia, Klein Constantia and Buitenverwachting. Their restaurants count among the best in South Africa. If you travel there, make reservations! Note that Klein Constantia once again produces the original "Constantia" in bottles shaped to resemble the old ones.

The laws and regulations are weaker in South Africa than in many European countries. There is no control over yield, planting density, irrigation, use of fertilizers or pest control. Blending wines from cultivars different from the one mentioned on the label is allowed: up to 15% for exports, more for the local market.

Several European and American wineries now have investments in South Africa. A number of spectacularwines from cultivars such as the Cabernet Sauvignon, Pinotage, Merlot, Shiraz, Chardonnay and Steen (Chenin Blanc) are now available on the world market. But much lower-quality wines are also lurking among them.

Figures 115-116: The wine regions of South Africa are clustered around Cape Town (maps: Kristin Reid).

AUSTRALIA

The Australian wine industry begins to recover shortly after the end of World War II. However, in the first few decades, volume matters more than quality. Until 1970 most Australian wines are fortified and, like in South Africa and the US, improperly labeled "sherry" and "port."[23] In the late 1970s and early 1980s the production of dry table wines increases substantially. This development could have a correlation with the 1976 wine tasting in Paris. New vineyards are planted with high-quality cultivars in selected locations. Cabernet Sauvignon, Shiraz, and Chardonnay are widespread. State-of-the-art technology, first imported then developed locally, is now omnipresent and impressive.

---

23. The word "improperly" is not meant to suggest that these fortified wines are bad. In fact, some of them are excellent. But "sherry" and "port" refer to the wines from Jerez and Porto. The soil, climate, cultivars, yeast and other important parameters are different in Australia than in the Jerez region or the Douro Valley. Why force a comparison to products that are not comparable?

At first, the best wines are kept for the local market and only the lesser wines are exported. As a result, the international reputation of Australian wines remains lower than it should be for many years. This has since changed, and some of the best Australian wines are sold world-wide. However, the quality of the average wine is higher in Australia than in other countries.

Today, Australia has 29 wine regions: eight in Victoria, six in south-east New South Wales, one in Queensland south of Brisbane, eight in South Australia clustered around Adelaide, four in Western Australia near Perth, and two in Tasmania. While most amateurs are familiar with the Barossa and Hunter Valleys, and quality wines are now being produced almost everywhere.

The Australian appellation of origin system is the Label Integrity Program (LIP). It was created by the Australian Wine and Brandy Corporation and took effect with the 1990 vintage. The intent of the program is to create an audit trail from grape to bottle for any claim on the label of a bottle. The winemaker must keep records for seven years of the production and acquisition of grapes and other goods, and the manufacture, sale, and the disposal of wines, in a way that leaves an audit trail.

Figures 117-118: A few of the many wine regions of Australia (maps: Kristin Reid).

New Zealand

The development of the wine industry in New Zealand is somewhat slower than elsewhere. One reason is that, until recently, New Zealand has been struggling with the issue of prohibition. Strict liquor laws are still in place, but the situation is evolving.

The first wine in the well-known Marlborough region is produced in 1973. The Wine Institute of New Zealand is created in 1975, and wine dilution is illegal since 1980. The excess production in 1983 compels the government to organize a vine-pulling scheme. By 1986 almost one-quarter of New Zealand vines are uprooted. Since then, the trend has reversed and exports increased. In

1991, over 130 wineries export about one million gallons of wine. In 2000, 334 wineries export about four times as much.

Much of the wine production of New Zealand consists of dry white wines, in particular from the Sauvignon Blanc, Chardonnay, and Gewurztraminer cultivars. However, wines from the Pinot Noir, Riesling, Merlot and Cabernet Sauvignon are also produced, as well as some champagne-style sparkling wines. The wines from New Zealand are distinct and their quality is increasing.

Figures 119-120: The wine regions of New Zealand (maps: Kristin Reid).

CHAPTER 7. FINAL THOUGHTS

Ah! bouteille, ma mie, pourquoi vous videz-vous?
—Molière (1622-1673)

Wine is an important part of life since the dawn of Western civilization. Their histories are often intertwined. Political or economic changes, scientific or technological breakthroughs, as well as climatic variations or the arrival of new pests have profoundly affected the way wine is made, transported, aged, and drunk. There is no reason to believe that we have now reached any kind of steady state. In fact, it is safe to predict that more changes, hopefully beneficial, will take place.

We will never know the taste of the great wines of the past, such as Julius Caesar's *Falernum* or Sam Pepys' *Ho Bryan*. But these are the rare and expensive wines worth dreaming and writing about. But the everyday wines of ancient times would probably be considered undrinkable today. There is little doubt that the quality of today's average wine is much higher than in the past. Much of the improvement can be traced back to scientific and technological break-throughs. The understanding of viticulture, fermentation, yeast selection, wine chemistry, maturation, and aging has vastly increased in the past several decades. Yesterday's educated guess is today's quantitative science. Weather forecasting is much more reliable as well. With timely rainfall and sunshine, a skilled winemaker can produce wine that is either ready to drink — the current trend, at least in some countries — or able to age and improve with years. It is becoming difficult, albeit not impossible, to find truly bad wines.

On the other hand, our understanding of wine is far from complete. Over 400 chemicals have so far been identified in wine and their role is studied.[1] Beyond water, the most important components are *acids* (tartaric, malic, lactic,

---

1. B.F. Somerville, Today's Chemist **4**, 16 (1991).

acetic), *sugars* (mostly glucose and fructose), *alcohols* and *esters, sulphur dioxide* and *glycerin*. However, the chemical changes that occur during the aging of wine, especially over long periods of time, are not known except for the fact that entropy must play a role.

Wines that are capable of improving with age are made from "noble" cultivars. A few of the better-known ones include the Chardonnay, Sauvignon Blanc, or Viognier (in white), and the Cabernet Sauvignon, Merlot or Pinot Noir (in red). But there are many hundreds of others,[2] from the fabulous Nebbiolo, Sangiovese, or Tempranillo to the lesser-known Ruche or Xinomavro. There is a universe waiting to be discovered.

In order to benefit from aging, the wine made from noble grapes needs tannins, mostly from the skin and sometimes stem. How much tannin is present in the fruit depends a lot on the cultivar and the age of the vine. To extract tannins, the winemaker macerates the juice with the skins and pips, often for several days. Rapid juice extraction prevents the tannin and color from dissolving in the fermenting must. Tannin from grapes makes the young wine taste harsh, astringent. With age, the tannin slowly evolves into flavors and aromas. The wine becomes softer, more complex, and lasts longer in the mouth. On the other hand, wood tannin[3] from the oak barrel or oak chips[4] added to the wine is softer. It masks the harshness of a wine that is too young. It makes the wine ready to drink much earlier. Such a wine can have a much more pronounced "fruit," and the oak flavor often imparts a flavor compared to "vanilla," "butter," or even "coconut," depending on the type of oak. But a wine with too much oak has been compared to a strong coffee with too much sugar. How much is too much is of course a matter of taste. However, these "oaky" wines do not age as gracefully as the wines loaded with grape tannin. Wines with more grape tannin and less wood tannin mature better. And anyone with a craving for vanilla, buter and coconut might look for a bakery, not a Chardonnay.

The age of the vine is a very important factor as well, a fact duly noted by Thomas Jefferson while traveling through the French wine regions. Past the age of 30 or so, a vine produces fewer clusters. The grains are smaller and have a thicker skin. The result is less juice, more concentration, and more tannin. French regulations strictly limit the volume of wine that can be produced per acre. Any excess cannot be sold, even for distillation, thus encouraging quality. It is common to find century-old vines in Bordeaux, Burgundy, or Côtes du Rhône, but these are rare in other wine-producing regions. Younger vines produce more fruit.

---

2. J. Robinson, *Guide to Wine Grapes* (Oxford University Press, Oxford, 1996).
3. The presence of oak tannins in a wine jar has been detected in Crete in the 2nd millennium BCE.
4. This is commonly done in California, for example, but is illegal in France.

To the best of my knowledge, the oldest living vine in the world is "The Great Vine." It grows comfortably in its private greenhouse at Hampton Court Palace, near London. It is the former residence of British kings, most notably Henry VIII. The vine was planted in 1768 by Lancelot "Capability" Brown. He was the Surveyor to King George III's Gardens and Waters. The cutting came from an old vine in Valentine, Essex. This vine produces annually some 600 pounds of sweet Black Hamburgh dessert grapes.

Figure 121: Recent photograph of the Great Vine showing some clusters of grapes (copyright: Historic Royal Palaces,(photograph: Nick Guttridge).

Not all wines are capable of aging or should be aged. Obviously, some wines are designed to be drunk young, while fresh and vibrant such as the Portuguese Vinhos Verdes, or the Italian Moscato d'Asti. But the wines from noble cultivars and older vines, that undergo extensive maceration, then mature in barrels and bottled without filtering out the tannin, benefit enormously from aging in bottles. Their color changes with time, as red wines lose pigments and white wines get darker because of oxygenation.

Figure 122: From left to right, the 1971, 1975, 1989, and 1990 vintages of the fabulous "Cuvée Madame" of Chateau Coutet, a first growth of Sauternes (photo SKE).

Properly aging wine is easy for those lucky enough to have a good wine cellar. A good wine cellar is dark and cool, with slow temperature fluctuations. The ideal temperature is probably around 65F. The humidity should be high, about 70%; otherwise the corks dry and shrink on the side exposed to the air. In an arid area, one way to achieve a good humidity is by watering 6 inches of gravel on the floor (gravel has a high surface-to-volume ratio). In any case, monitoring the temperature and the humidity is necessary. Last but not least, the cellar must be free of odors. An oil furnace or a bucket of paint nearby will surely and quickly ruin the wine. The alternative to a cellar is a temperature and humidity controlled cabinet.

Wine in a small bottle ages faster than in a large bottle. The capacity of a standard wine bottle is 0.75 liters (0.198 gallons). The capacity (in liters) of larger bottles is as follows. The *Magnum* is 1.5 (2 bottles); the *Jeroboam* is 3.0 (4 bottles) in Champagne and 4.5 (6 bottles) in Bordeaux; the *Rehoboam* is 4.5 (6 bottles) in Champagne; the *Methuselah* (Champagne) or *Imperial* (elsewhere) is 6.0 (8 bottles); the *Salmanazar* is 9.0 (12 bottles); the *Balthazar* is 12.0 (16 bottles); and the *Nebuchadnezzar* is 15.0 (20 standard bottles).

In the 1980s the prices of top-name wines, then those of lesser-name wines, dramatically increases. In 1986, a 1784 bottle of Chateau d'Yquem with the initials Th.J. engraved[5] is sold for $56,628. In 1985, a 1787 Chateau Lafite goes for

---

5. While Jefferson did request from Ch. Yquem that cases of wine be labeled GW (for George Washington) or ThJ (for himself), there is no evidence that he requested that individual bottles be engraved with his initials. This expensive procedure is uncharacteristic.

$156,450. A few years later, seven Methuselah of 1985 Romanée Conti is sold at Sotheby's for $225,000. This is about $800 per 1.5dl glass. Such sales drive the price of all brand-name wines upward, as these bottles become collector's items. Today's "top" brand-name wines are reserved to a very wealthy clientele indeed. But there are many wonderful buys from lesser-known countries or cultivars. The more you know, the better off you are. It pays to be curious. Portugal, South Africa, Argentina, and even Mexico for example produce some excellent wines. Chateau Musar is the best-known Lebanese wine but it is not the only winery near the Bekaa Valley. Such wines are much easier to find today than ten years ago.

Figure 123: The Chateau Ksara winery in the Bekaa valley (photo Lisa Rezzonico).

Statistics about the world-wide production and consumption of wine are available from the Wine Institute. The largest world producer of wine in 2001 was France, with over 53.4 million hectoliters (1 M hl = 26.4 million gallons). A close second is Italy, with 50.1. Then come Spain (30.5), the United States (21.3), Argentina (15.8), China (10.8), Australia (10.2), Germany (8.9), Portugal (7.8), South Africa (6.5). These numbers fluctuate from year to year, with climatic conditions and other factors. The newcomer in this "Top 10" list is China, where the wine production has more than tripled since 1997, mostly in the north-east of the country. Australia is also experiencing substantial growth in this area.

As far as per capita consumption, the number one country in the world is Luxembourg, with an average of over 59 liters per year for every man, woman, and child. Close seconds are France (57) and Italy (53). Then come Portugal, Croatia, Switzerland, Spain, and Argentina. The United States is 34th on the list, just below Canada, with less than 9 liters per capita. These statistics provide a useful snapshot but not a complete picture. In India for example, where the annual per capita consumption is probably measured in glasses rather than liters, wineries such as Sula Vineyards east of Bombay (est. 2000) cannot keep up with the demand. While the acreage planted with vines in "old world" countries remains rather constant, the acreage in "new world" countries is increasing rapidly.

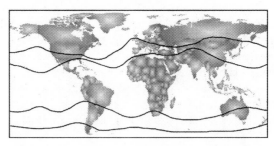

Figure 124: Except for the vineyards of Canada and India, most of today's wine regions lie between the 10°C and 20°C isotherms (map: Kristin Reid).

Globalization is changing the world of wine. In 1979, *Opus One* was one of the first international joint venture, involving Baron Philippe de Rothschild in Bordeaux and Robert Mondavi in Napa. Many French-Californian ventures have been successful since, some involving champagne houses. Today, moderately-priced California champagnes rival much more expensive French ones. Some of them even age nicely. Lafite-Rothschild has substantial holdings in Chile, Los Vascos for example, and Portugal. Antinori purchased vineyards in South Africa. The list goes on and on.

At present, there is no uniform level of government supervision of viti-culture, winemaking, or labeling in the world. On one hand, the traditional European countries such as France, Italy, or Spain have very strict government controls. Precise geographical locations, yields, allowed cultivars, pruning methods, vinification techniques — everything is controlled in order to provide guarantees of origin and quality. Uniform European standards are increasingly being developed, for better or worse. One the other hand, government regula-tions are loose in South Africa, Australia, and California. Hardly any regulations at all exist in many other countries.

Today, a war of sorts is being fought about corks. The best corks in the world come from Portugal, and also from Spain and Sardinia. A cork oak lives an average of 150 years, but its bark is thick enough to make cork only past the age of 30. Once it has been removed, the tree needs about ten years to develop a new thick layer of cork. The removed slab is left in open air for about one year before the corks are punched out, washed, and any trace of dust removed. Finally, they get a thin coat of silicone and are ready for use. Corks are expensive, and the demand far exceeds the production. Much cheaper stoppers are obtained by gluing together the bits of cork that remain after good corks have been punched out of a piece of bark.

Although many people believe that a high quality cork is the best way to stopper a bottle for aging, corks also have critics. It is true that an occasional bad cork gives a bad taste to the wine. This is very rare when quality corks are used, but much more common when using lower-quality composites. The chemical responsible for most of the problem is called "246-TCA" (*2, 4, 6-trichloroanisole*). A cork can of course also be affected by parasites or fungi. Some writers claim that nearly 10% of wine bottles have a "cork" problem. This is not my experience, but this is a matter of how sensitive one's nose is.

Many winemakers are considering alternatives to corks. The simplest one is the twist-off cap. Synthetic corks are being tested by many wineries, but lawsuits have resulted from thousands of corks stuck so tightly in bottles that it was nearly impossible to open them. Finding the perfect replacement for natural corks is still in the future. Nobody knows how a wine with a synthetic cork will age. Wines can age well over several decades with a natural cork. There is a good probability that top quality corks will still be used for those wines that benefit from long aging. On the other hand, the wines that do not need time in the cellar do not require such corks. Dear Bacchus, may screwtops and corks that look and feel like plastic be only a temporary solution.

In any case, today is a good day to be a wine lover. The best advice I can give is not to follow too closely the recommendations of others but to be curious and learn from wines made with little-known cultivars. The best way to enjoy a wine is to be able to compare it to many other wines. Trust your own nose and palate. Your taste will evolve with time, and the journey will be most captivating. Curious is better than right or wrong.

When Ptolemy, now long ago,
Believed the Earth stood still,
He never would have blundered so
Had he but drunk his fill.
He'd then have felt it circulate
And would have learnt to say:
The true way to investigate
Is to drink a bottle a day.

— author unknown, reported in Augustus de Morgan's Budget of Paradoxes (1866)

Appendix A: Cuvées des Hospices de Beaune

Note: Donations of vineyards to the Hospices de Beaune still occur today.

AUXEY-DURESSES — cuvée BOILLOT: Antoinette BOILLOT donated her vineyards in Auxey-Duresses, Meursault and Volnay in 1898.

BATARD MONTRACHET — cuvée DAMES DE FLANDRES: In 1989, the Hospices purchased a fraction of this Grand Cru vineyard and named it "Dames de Flandres" as the Sisters of the Hôtel-Dieu were known.

BEAUNE — cuvée NICOLAS ROLIN: Nicolas Rolin was the chancellor of Philippe le Good and the founder of the Hôtel-Dieu. The amount of wine sold as "Nicolas Rolin" increased in 1963 with a donation from the widow Maurice PALLAGOIX, in memory of her husband.

BEAUNE — cuvée GUIGONE DE SALINS: Named after the wife of Nicolas Rolin who was very dedicated to the Hôtel-Dieu.

BEAUNE — cuvée ROUSSEAU DESLANDES: Named after the husband and wife who founded the Hospice de la Charité in Beaune three centuries ago.

BEAUNE — cuvée DES DAMES HOSPITALIÈRES: For over 500 years, the Sisters "Dames Hospitalières" have dedicated their lives to the poor and the sick.

BEAUNE — cuvée BETAULT: Hugues BETAULT (adviser, secretary of the king) and his brother established the infirmary and the care room (salle Saint-Louis) in 1615.

BEAUNE — cuvée BRUNET: Five members of the family Brunet made donations to the benefit of the sick.

BEAUNE — cuvée Maurice DROUHIN: Maurice DROUHIN, administrator then vice-president of the Hospices from 1941 to 1955, donated an important vineyard within the Beaune appellation.

BEAUNE — cuvée CYROT CHAUDRON: In 1979, CYROT CHAUDRON and his wife donated vineyards in Beaune and Pommard

BEAUNE — cuvée CLOS DES AVAUX: This appellation consists of vineyards that belonged to the Hospice de la Charité before the French Revolution (1789).

CLOS DE LA ROCHE — cuvée Georges KRITTER: The Hospices de BEAUNE purchased in 1991 a fragment of this Grand Cru vineyard using a donation from Mrs. Georges KRITTER.

CLOS DE LA ROCHE — cuvée CYROT CHAUDRON: Mr. and Mrs. CYROT CHAUDRON made a donation in 1991. It allowed the Hospices to increase the size of the vineyard donated by Mrs. Georges KRITTER.

CORTON — cuvée Charlotte DUMAY: Donated part of a vineyard in Aloxe-Corton in 1584.

CORTON — cuvée Docteur PESTE: The Baronne du Bay gave her vineyards in Aloxe-Corton. In 1965, the property was enlarged with a gift from Marcel FOURNIER in memory of her husband, and her uncle and aunt, THEVENOT-BUSSIERE.

CORTON CHARLEMAGNE — cuvée François de SALINS: In 1745, François de SALINS left a legacy of his vineyard in Aloxe-Corton and Savigny.

CORTON VERGENNES — cuvée Paul CHANSON: Part of a vineyard donated by Paul Chanson in 1974.

MAZIS CHAMBERTIN — cuvée Madeleine COLLIGNON: In memory of Mr. and Mrs. Marcel THOMAS-COLLIGNON.

MEURSAULT — cuvée Jehan HUMBLOT: This notary from Beaune gave his property of Laborde-au-Bureau in 1600.

MEURSAULT — cuvée LOPPIN: Members of this family donated money, buildings, other gifts.

MEURSAULT — cuvée GOUREAU: Miss GOUREAU donated properties in Masse, Corcelles, Mimande, Chaudenay, Ebaty, Demigny.

MEURSAULT CHARMES — cuvée Louis de BAHEZRE de LANLAY: This former inspector of telegraphs donated his entire fortune to the Hospices.

MEURSAULT CHARMES — cuvée Albert GRIVAULT: Mr. and Mrs. GRIVAULT donated a vineyard in 1914.

MEURSAULT GENEVRIÈRES — cuvée BAUDOT: The scientist and antiquarian of Burgundy (and his family) donated a collection of antiquities and art in 1880 (the collection was later sold).

MEURSAULT GENEVRIERES — cuvée Philippe le BON: Named after the duke of Burgundy who allowed (and helped) his chancellor create the Hospices.

MONTHELIE — cuvée Jacques LEBELIN: Mr. and Mrs. LEBELIN donated a large sum.

PERNAND VERGELESSES — cuvée RAMEAU LAMAROSSE: She was the last descendent of an old Burgundy family. She donated her house and vineyards.

POMMARD — cuvée DES DAMES DE LA CHARITÉ: The Sisters of Charity dedicated their lives to the care of the elderly and orphans. Many Sisters donated personal belongings.

POMMARD — cuvée BILLARDET: Drs. Billardet organized the surgical ward. Their daughters and grand-daughters also contributed.

POMMARD — cuvée Raymond CYROT et cuvée Suzanne CHAUDRON: In 1979, Mr. and Mrs. CYROT CHAUDRON donated fine vineyards in Beaune and Pommard.

POUILLY FUISSÉ — cuvée Françoise POISARD: In 1994, Françoise POISARD left a legacy of two houses as well as land and vineyards, of which ten acres in Pouilly Fuissé.

SAVIGNY Les BEAUNE — cuvée Arthur GIRARD, who donated a part of his estate to the Hospices in 1936.

SAVIGNY Les BEAUNE — cuvée FORNERET: A noted family from Beaune, who donated a property in Savigny et Pernand.

SAVIGNY Les BEAUNE — cuvée FOUQUERAND: Denis Antoine FOUQUERAND made a donation in 1844 and his wife, Charlotte-Claudine BONNARD, already had written a will benefiting the Hospices in 1832.

VOLNAY — cuvée BLONDEAU: François BLONDEAU donated properties in Volnay, Pommard, Monthélie, Bligny, Beaune.

VOLNAY — cuvée Général MUTEAU: Donated the property of Laborde au Château.

VOLNAY SANTENOTS — cuvée Jehan de Massol: Counsillor of the King at the Parliament in Beaune, left his belongings, including vineyards in Meursault, Demigny and Travoisy.

VOLNAY SANTENOTS — cuvée GAUVAIN: In 1804, Bernard GAUVAIN donated all his estate. His widow donated her hotel in Beaune and her land in Chivres and Laborde au Bureau.

Appendix B: French Classifications of Bordeaux Wines

The earliest (1855) classification of the best Bordeaux wines was carried out by the Bordeaux Syndicate of Wine Brokers. The prices fetched by the wines of various Chateaux were the basis for the ranking. The approach was later used for other classifications.

The Classification of 1855

The name of each château is followed by its district (commune). The first growths are listed in the official order. The other wines are listed in alphabetical order. The number in parenthesis associated with each wine refers to the order of the ranking in the original document.

RED WINES

Premiers Crus

Lafite-Rothschild (Pauillac)
Latour (Pauillac)
Margaux (Margaux)
Mouton-Rothschild (Pauillac)
Haut-Brion (Pessac, Graves)

Deuxiemes Crus

Brane-Cantenac (Cantenac) (9)
Cos d'Estournel (Saint-Estèphe) (13)
Ducru-Beaucaillou (Saint-Julien) (12)
Durfort-Vivens (Margaux) (6)
Gruaud-Larose (Saint-Julien) (7)
Lascombes (Margaux) (8)
Léoville-Barton (Saint-Julien) (5)
Léoville-Las-Cases (Saint-Julien) (3)
Léoville-Poyferré (Saint-Julien) (4)

Montrose (Saint-Estèphe) (14)

Pichon-Longueville (Baron) (Pauillac) (10)

Pichon-Longueville, Comtesse-de-Lalande (Pauillac) (11)

Rausan-Ségla (Margaux) (1)

Rauzan-Gassies (Margaux) (2)

Troisiemes Crus

Boyd-Cantenac (Cantenac) (8)

Calon-Ségur (Saint-Estèphe) (12)

Cantenac-Brown (Cantenac) (7)

Desmirail[6] (Cantenac) (11)

Ferrière[7] (Margaux) (13)

Giscours (Labarde) (5)

Issan (Cantenac) (2)

Kirwan (Cantenac) (1)

Lagrange (Saint-Julien) (3)

La Lagune (Ludon) (10)

Langoa-Barton (Saint-Julien) (4)

Malescot-Saint-Exupéry (Margaux) (6)

Marquis-d'Alesme-Becker (Margaux) (14)

Palmer (Cantenac) (9)

Quatriemes Crus

Beychevelle (Saint-Julien) (8)

Branaire-Ducru (Saint-Julien) (3)

Duhart-Milon-Rothschild (Pauillac) (4)

Lafont-Rochet (Saint-Estèphe) (7)

La Tour-Carnet (Saint-Laurent) (6)

Marquis-de-Terme (Margaux) (10)

Pouget (Cantenac) (5)

Prieuré-Lichine (Cantenac) (9)

Saint-Pierre (Saint-Julien) (1)

Talbot (Saint-Julien) (2)

Cinquiemes Crus

Batailley (Pauillac) (2)

Belgrave (Saint-Laurent) (13)

Camensac (Saint-Laurent) (14)

Cantemerle (Macau) (18)

Clerc-Milon (Pauillac) (16)

Cos Labory (Saint-Estèphe)} (15)

Croizet-Bages (Pauillac) (17)

Dauzac (Labarde) (8)

Du Tertre (Arsac) (10)

Grand-Puy-Ducasse (Pauillac) (5)

Grand-Puy-Lacoste (Pauillac) (4)

Haut-Bages-Libéral (Pauillac) (11)

Haut-Batailley (Pauillac) (3)

Lynch-Bages (Pauillac) (6)

Lynch-Moussas (Pauillac) (7)

Mouton-Baronne-Philippe[8] (Pauillac) (9)

Pédesclaux (Pauillac) (12)

Pontet-Canet (Pauillac) (1)

WHITE WINES

Grand Premier Cru

d'Yquem (Sauternes)

Premiers Crus

Climens (Barsac) (7)

Clos Haut-Peyraguey (Bommes) (3)

Coutet (Barsac) (6)

Guiraud (Sauternes) (8)

Lafaurie-Peyraguey (Bommes) (2)

La Tour Blanche (Bommes) (1)

---

6. Château Desmirail disappeared early in the 20th century, but is again available since 1981.

7. Château Ferrière is no longer on the market.

8. Mouton-d'Armailhacq until 1956, and was renamed Mouton-Baron-Philippe prior to the death in 1975 of Baron Philippe's second wife, Pauline.

Rabaud-Promis (Bommes) (10)
Rayne-Vigneau (Bommes) (4)
Rieussec (Fargues) (9)
Sigalas-Rabaud (Bommes) (11)
Suduiraut (Preignac) (5)

Deuxiemes Crus

Broustet (Barsac) (6)
Caillou (Barsac) (8)
d'Arche (Sauternes) (4)
de Malle (Preignac) (10)
Doisy-Daëne, -Dubroca (Barsac) (2)
Doisy-Védrines (Barsac) (3)
Filhot (Sauternes) (5)
Lamothe (Despujols, Guignard)
    (Sauternes) (12)
Myrat (Barsac) (1)
Nairac (Barsac) (7)
Romer-du-Hayot (Bommes) (11)
Suau (Barsac) (9)

THE CLASSIFICATION OF 1953:
RED GRAVES

Bouscaut (Cadaujac)
Carbonnieux (Léognan)
Domaine de Chevalier (Léognan)
Fieuzal (Léognan)
Haut-Bailly (Léognan)
La Mission-Haut-Brion (Pessac)
Latour-Haut-Brion (Pessac)
La Tour-Martillac (Léognan)
Malartic-Lagravière (Léognan)
Olivier (Léognan)
Pape-Clément (Pessac)
Smith-Haut-Lafite (Léognan)

THE CLASSIFICATION OF 1959:
WHITE GRAVES

Bouscaut (Cadaujac)
Carbonnieux (Léognan)
Couhins-Lurton (Léognan)
Domaine de Chevalier (Léognan)
La Tour Martillac (Léognan)
Laville-Haut-Brion (Pessac)
Malartic-Lagravière (Léognan)
Olivier (Léognan)

THE CLASSIFICATION OF 1955: SAINT
EMILION *(Revised May 23, 1986)*

Premiers Grand Crus Classes A

Ausone
Cheval-Blanc

Premiers Grand Crus Classes B

Beauséjour (Duffau-Lagarosse)
Belair
Canon
Clos Fourtet
Figeac
La Gaffelière
Magdelaine
Pavie
Trottevieille

Grands Crus Classes

Balestard La Tonelle
Beauséjour
Bellevue
Bergat
Berliquet
Cadet-Piola
Canon-La-Gaffelière
Cap de Mourlin

Chauvin

Clos de l'Oratoire

Clos des Jacobins

Clos la Madeleine

Clos Saint-Martin

Corbin

Corbin-Michotte

Coutet

Couvent des Jacobins

Croque Michotte

Curé Bon La Madeleine

Dassault

Faurie de Souchard

Fonplegade

Fonroque

Franc-Mayne

Grand-Barrail-Lamarzelle-Figeac

Grand Corbin

Grand Corbin-Despagne

Grand Mayne

Grand Pontet

Guadet Saint-Julien

Haut Corbin

Haut Sarpe

La Clotte

La Clusière

La Dominique

Lamarzelle

L'Angélus

Laniote

Larcis-Ducasse

Larmande

Laroze

L'Arrosée

La Serre

La Tour du Pin Figeac

La Tour-Figeac

Le Châtelet

Le Prieuré

Matras

Mauvezin

Moulin du Cadet

Pavie-Decesse

Pavie-Macquin

Pavillon-Cadet

Petit-Faurie-de-Soutard

Ripeau

Sansonnet

Saint-Georges Côte Pavie

Soutard

Tertre Daugay

Trimoulet

Troplong-Mondot

Villemaurine

Yon-Figeac

Appendix C: Modern Classifications

The 1855 classification was based purely on the price customers were willing to pay for a given wine. Some records dated back as much as a century. This approach has been extended by Orley Ashenfelter. He developed new and objective rankings using records from wine auctions held throughout the world. The classification below was published in Liquid Assets (Dec. 1997, reproduced with permission). It is based on over 10,000 transactions in London for the period May 1994 to December 1996, and excludes the wines less than 10 years old when purchased. The reference wine is Château Lafite-Rothschild, the price of which is normalized to 100. Not surprisingly, major differences exist between this new classification and the old ones.

The same approach was used to rank the California Cabernet Sauvignons in 1996. The basis is the price fetched at auctions from 1968 to 1985. The price fetched by the Beaulieu Vineyards Private Reserve is normalized to 100. This classification follows that of the Bordeaux reds.

THE CLASSIFICATION OF 1997:
RED BORDEAUX

708% Le Pin (Pomerol)
369% Pétrus (Pomerol)
160% Lafleur (Pomerol)
129% Mouton-Rothschild (Pauillac)
121% Cheval Blanc (St. Emilion)
113% Latour (Pauillac)
105% Margaux (Margaux)
100% Lafite-Rothschild (Pauillac)
85% Mission-Haut-Brion (Graves)
78% Haut-Brion (Graves)
75% Ausone (St. Emilion)
71% Trotanoy (Pomerol)

66% L'Evangile (Pomerol)
59% Pichon-Longueville (Pauillac)
56% Certan de May (Pomerol)
55% Palmer (Margaux)
52% Leoville-Las-Cases (St. Julien)
50% La Fleur Pétrus (Pomerol)
50% Lynch Bages (Pauillac)
47% Les Forts de Latour (Pauillac)
47% La Conseillante (Pomerol)
47% Latour a Pomerol (Pomerol)
46% Figeac (St. Emilion)
44% Le Tertre-Roteboeuf (St. Emilion)
44% Cos d'Estournel (St. Estèphe)
44% La Tour Haut-Brion (Graves)

43% Vieux Chateau Certan (Pomerol)	22% Sociando Mallet (Médoc)
42% Ducru Beaucaillou (St. Julien)	22% Pape Clement (Graves)
40% Domaine de Chevalier (Léognan)	22% D'Issan (Margaux)
40% L'Eglise-Clinet (Pomerol)	22% Cantenac Brown (Margaux)
37% Gruaud Larose (St. Julien)	22% Cantemerle (Macau)
36% Canon (S. Emilion)	21% Belair (St. Emilion)
34% Giscours (Margaux)	21% Duhart-Milon-Rothschild (Pauillac)
32% Petit Village (Pomerol)	
32% Talbot (St. Julien)	21% Brane-Cantenac (Margaux)
32% Pavillon Rouge (Margaux)	21% Batailley (Pauillac)
31% Montrose (St. Estèphe)	21% Clos du Marquis (St. Julien)
31% Pavie (St. Emilion)	21% Certan-Giraud (Pomerol)
31% Magdelaine (St. Emilion)	21% De Sales (Pomerol)
31% Beychevelle (St. Julien)	20% Fieuzal (Graves)
30% Léoville Barton (St. Julien)	20% Clerc-Milon (Pauillac)
30% Grand Puy Lacoste (Pauillac)	20% Labergorce-Zede (Margaux)
30% La Lagune (Ludon)	20% L'Angelus (St. Emilion)
29% Moulin de Carruades (Pauillac)	20% Haut-Bages-Liberal (Pauillac)
29% Bon Pasteur (Pomerol)	20% Meyney (St. Estèphe)
28% Clinet (Pomerol)	20% Prieuré-Lichine (Margaux)
28% L'Arrosée (St. Emilion)	20% Gazin (Pomerol)
27% Grave-Trigant-de-Boisset (Pomerol)	20% Poujeaux (Moulis)
	19% La-Croix-de-Gay (Pomerol)
25% Haut Marbuzet (St. Estèphe)	19% L'Enclos (Pomerol)
24% Rausan Ségla (Margaux)	19% D'Angludet (Margaux)
24% Haut Bailly (Graves)	19% De Pez (St. Estèphe)
24% Chasse Spleen (Moulis)	19% Lagrange (St. Julien)
24% Baron Pichon Longueville (Pauillac)	19% Canon La Gaffeliere (St. Emilion)
	19% Haut-Bages-Averous (Pauillac)
24% Leoville Poyferré (St. Julien)	19% Pavie-Decesse (St. Emilion)
24% Saint Pierre (St. Julien)	19% Dufort-Vivens (Margaux)
23% Branaire Ducru (St. Julien)	18% Grand-Puy-Ducasse (Pauillac)
23% Le Gay (Pomerol)	18% Les Ormes de Pez (St. Estèphe)
23% Langoa Barton (St. Julien)	18% Rauzan Gassies (Margaux)
23% La Dominique (St. Emilion)	18% Boyd-Cantenac (Margaux)
23% Calon Ségur (St. Estèphe)	18% Larrivet-Haut-Brion (Graves)
23% La Gaffeliere (St. Emilion)	18% Malescot-St-Exupéry (Margaux)
23% Haut Batailley (Pauillac)	18% Croizet-Bages (Pauillac)
23% Mouton Baronne Philippe (Pauillac)	18% Pontet Canet (Pauillac)
	18% Smith-Haut-Lafite (Graves)
22% Gloria (St. Julien)	17% Potensac (Médoc)
22% Lascombe (Margaux)	17% Nenin (Pomerol)
22% Larmande (St. Emilion)	17% Siran (Margaux)

17%   Clos Rene (Pomerol)
17%   Cissac (Cissac)
17%   Soutard (St. Emilion)
17%   La Louvière Rouge (Leognan)
17%   Marquis-de-Terme (Margaux)
16%   La Pointe (Pomerol)
16%   Gressier-Grand-Poujeaux (Moulis)
16%   Camensac (St. Laurent)
16%   Marquis d'Alesme-Becker (Margaux)
16%   Du Tertre (Margaux)
15%   Domaine de L'Eglise (Pomerol)
15%   Clos du Clocher (Pomerol)
15%   Trottevieille (St. Emilion)
15%   La Tour de Mons (Margaux)
15%   La Tour Figeac (St. Emilion)
15%   Coufran (Haut Médoc)
15%   Lafont-Rochet (St. Estèphe)
15%   La Tour-St-Bonnet (Médoc)
15%   Malartic-Lagraviere (Leognan)
14%   Kirwan (Margaux)
14%   La Tour-de-By (Médoc)
14%   Beauregard (Pomerol)
14%   Carbonnieux (Graves)
14%   Cure Bon La Madeleine (St. Emilion)
14%   Fombrauge (St. Emilion)
13%   Phelan Ségur (St. Estèphe)
13%   Lalande-Borie (St. Julien)
13%   Beaumolnt (Médoc)
13%   Lynch-Moussas (Pauillac)
12%   Grand Mayne (St. Emilion)
12%   Patache d'Aux (Médoc)
12%   Larozé (St. Emilion)
12%   Cos-Labory (St. Estephe)
11%   Liversan (Haut Médoc)

THE CLASSIFICATION OF 1996:
CALIFORNIA CABERNET SAUVIGNON

366% Caymus Special Selection (Napa)
242% Opus I (Napa)

239% Stag's Leap Wine Cellars Cask 23 (Napa)
215% Dunn Howell Mountain (Napa)
206% Heitz Martha's Vineyard (Napa)
172% Spottswoode (Napa)
155% Ridge Monte Bello (Cupertino, SF)
150% Silver Oak (Napa)
142% Dunn (Napa)
141% Beringer Reserve (Napa)
139% Chateau Montelena (Napa)
129% Dominus (Napa)
119% Silver Oak (Alexander Valley)
114% Joseph Phelps Insignia (Napa)
114% Forman (Napa)
112% Robert Mondavi Reserve (Napa)
101% Heitz Bella Oaks (Napa)
100% Beaulieu Vineyards Private Reserve (Napa)
99%   Duckhorn (Napa)
95%   Caymus Estate (Napa)
95%   Groth (Napa)
94%   Mayacamas (Napa/Sonoma)
94%   Stag's Leap Wine Cellars SLV (Napa)
92%   Jordan (Sonoma)
69%   Sterling Reserve (Napa)
65%   Clos du Val (Napa)
63%   Freemark Abbey Bosch (Napa)
61%   William Hill Reserve (Napa)
56%   Inglenook Reserve Cask (Madera)
56%   Carmenet (Sonoma)
54%   Heitz (Napa)
53%   Chapelet (Napa)
48%   Ridge York Creek (Napa)
47%   Joseph Phelps (Napa)
41%   Sterling (Napa)
41%   Robert Mondavi (Napa)
33%   Charles Krug Vintage Select (Napa)

Appendix D: Grand Crus of Alsace, Burgundy, Chablis

The French AOC system relates a wine to its geographical origin. The wines belonging to the highest category have only the name of the vineyard on their label. These "Grand Cru" wines are the best. Note that in Bordeaux, "Grand Cru" has a different meaning. Only a few French wine regions have Grand Cru wines.

Grand Crus of Alsace

Bas-Rhin

Altenberg de Bergbieten
Bruderthal
Engelberg
Frankstein
Kastelberg
Kirchberg de Barr
Moenchberg
Muenchberg
Praelatenberg
Steinklotz
Winzenberg

Haut-Rhin

Altenberg de Bergheim
Altenberg de Wolxheim
Brand
Eichberg
Florimont
Froehn
Furstentum
Geisberg
Gloeckelberg
Goldert
Hatschbourg
Hengst
Kanzlerberg
Kessler
Kirchberg de Ribeauvillé
Kitterlé
Mambourg
Mandelberg
Marckrain
Ollwiller
Osterberg

Pfersigberg
Pfingstberg
Rangen
Rosacker
Schlossberg
Schoenenberg
Sommerberg
Sonnenglanz
Spiegel
Sporen
Steinert
Steingrubler
Vorbourg
Wiebelsberg
Wineck-Schlossberg
Zinnkoepflé
Zotzenberg

La Tâche
Latricières-Chambertin
Mazis-Chambertin
Mazoyères-Chambertin
Musigny
Richebourg
Romanée-Conti
Romanée-St-Vivant
Ruchottes Chambertin

GRAND CRUS OF CHABLIS

Blanchot
Bougros
Grenouilles
Les Clos
Preuses
Valmur
Vaudesir

GRAND CRUS OF BURGUNDY

Cotes de Beaune

Bâtard-Montrachet
Bienvenues-Bâtard-Montrachet
Chevalier-Montrachet
Corton
Corton-Charlemagne
Criots-Bâtard-Montrachet
Montrachet

Cotes de Nuits

Bonnes Mares
Chambertin
Chambertin Clos de Bèze
Chapelle-Chambertin
Charmes-Chambertin
Clos de la Roche
Clos de Tart
Clos de Vougeot
Clos des Lambrays
Clos Saint-Denis
Echézeaux
Grands-Echézeaux
Griotte-Chambertin
La Grande Rue
La Romanée

BIBLIOGRAPHY

Aghion I., Barbillon C., and Lissarrague F., *Gods and Heroes of Classical Antiquity* (Flammarion, Paris, 1994).

Anderson B., *The Wines of Italy* (Simon and Schuster, New York, 1992).

Ashenfelter O., *The Wine Educator* 1 (1), 3 (1989).

Barbero A., *Charlemagne, Father of a Continent* (University of California Press, Berkeley, 2000).

Behr E., *Prohibition* (Arcade, New York, 1996).

Benson J. and Mackenzie A., *Sauternes* (Sotheby's, London, 1990).

de Blij H.J., *Wine Regions of the Southern Hemisphere* (Rowman & Allanheld, New Jersey, 1985).

Brennan T., Burgundy to Champagne: the Wine Trade in Early Modern France (Johns Hopkins, Baltimore, 1997).

Clough A.H. and Dryden J. (translated) *Plutarch: The Lives of the Noble Grecians and Romans* (Modern Library, New York, 1932).

Cobbold D. and Hurlin P., *The Great Vines and Vintages* (Chartwell Books, New Jersey, 1997).

Dalby A., *Bacchus: A Biography* (Getty, Los Angeles, 2003).

Dallas P., *Italian Wines* (Faber and Faber, London, 1989).

Davies J., *The Celts* (Cassell, London, 2002).

Dillon P., *Gin: The Much-Lamented Death of Madam Geneva* (Justin, Charles, & Co., Boston, 2003).

Echikson T., *Noble Rot*. Norton, New York, 2004).

Fagan B., *The Little Ice Age* (Basic Books, New York, 2000).

Faith N., *The Story of Champagne* (Hamish-Hamilton, London, 1988).

Ferguson N., *The House of Rothschild* (Penguin, 1998).

Fitzgerald E. (editor), *The Rubáiyát of Omar Khayyám*, fifth edition (Dover, 1990).

Fleming S.J., *Vinum* (Art Flair, Glenn Mills, 2001).

Franke P.R. and Marathaki I., *Wine and Coins in Ancient Greece* (The Hatzimichalis Estate, Athens, 1999).

Gabler J.M., *The Wines and Travels of Thomas Jefferson* (Bacchus Press, Baltimore, 1995).

Gulick C.B. (editor) *Athenaeus:* Deipnosophistai (Loeb Classical Library, Cambridge, 1928).

Hanson A., *Burgundy* (Faber and Faber, London, 1982).

Hardy T.K. and Roden M., *Pictorial Atlas of North American Wines* (Grape Vision, Pt Melbourne, 1988).

Jamieson I., *German Wines* (Faber and Faber, London, 1991).

Jobe J. (editor), *The Great Book of Wine* (Galahad, New York, 1982).

Johnson H., *Vintage* (Simon and Schuster, New York, 1989).

Kennedy J., *Coca Exotica* (Fairleigh Dickinson University Press, Rutherford, 1985).

Kladstrup D. and Kladstrup P., *Wine and War* (Broadway Books, New York, 2001).

Kolpan S., Smith B.H., and Weiss M.A., *Exploring Wine* (Wiley, New York, 1996).

Kramer M., *Making Sense of Wine* (Running Press, Philadelphia, 2003).

Kurlansky M., *Cod* (Penguin, 1997).

Latham R. and Matthews W. (editors), *The Diary of Samuel Pepys*, edited by (Harper Collins, UC Berkeley Press, 2000).

Leroux-Dhuys J.F. and Gaud H., *Cistercian Abbey: history and architecture* (Könemann, Cologne, 1988).

Macaulay G.C. (translated) and Lateiner D.E. (revised) *Herodotus:The Histories,* (Barnes and Noble Classics, New York, 2004).

MacNeil K., *The Wine Bible* (Workman, New York, 2001).

Manessis N., *The Illustrated Greek Wine Book* (Olive Press, Corfu, 2000).

Mathieson N., *Port* (Chartwell Books, Edison NJ, 1999).

McGovern P.E., *Ancient Wine* (Princeton University Press, Princeton 2003).

McGovern P.E., Fleming S.J., Katz S.H. (editors), *The Origins and Ancient History of Wine* (Gordon & Breach, Amsterdam, 2000).

McCoy E., *The Emperor of Wine: the Rise of Robert M. Parker, Jr. and the Rein of American Taste* (Harper Collins, New York, 2005).

McWhirter K. and Metcalfe C., *Encyclopedia of Spanish and Portuguese Wines* (Fireside, Simon and Schuster, New York, 1991).

Meade M., *Eleanor of Aquitaine, a Biography* (Penguin, New York, 1991).

Norman R., *The Great Domaines of Burgundy* (Henry Holt, New York, 1996).

Oakes L. and Gahlin L., *Ancient Egypt* (Barnes and Noble, New York, 2003).

Parker R.M. Jr., *Bordeaux: A Consumer's Guide to the World's Finest Wines* (Simon and Schuster, New York, 1985).

Parker R.M. Jr., *Wine of the Rhone Valley* (Simon and Schuster, New York, 1997).

Parker R.M. Jr., *Burgundy* (Simon and Schuster, New York, 1990).

Peterson H., *The Great Illusion: An Informal History of Prohibition* (Greenwood Press, New York, 1968).

Phillips R., *A Short History of Wine* (Harper Collins, New York, 2000).

Pickthall M.M (translated), *The Glorious Qur'an* (Tahrike Tarsile Qur'an, Elmhurst, 1999).

Pinney T., *A History of Wine in America: From the Beginnings to Prohibition* (University of California Press, Berkeley, 1985).

Pinney T., *A History of Wine in America: From Prohibition to the Present* (University of California Press, Berkeley, 2005).

Rainbird G., *An Illustrated Guide to Wine* (Peerage Books, London, 1980).

Read J., *The Wines of Portugal* (Faber and Faber, London, 1987).

Robinson J. (editor), *The Oxford Companion to Wine* (Oxford U. Press, New York, 1994).

Robinson J., *Guide to Wine Grapes* (Oxford University Press, Oxford, 1996).

Russell P., *Prince Henry "The Navigator," a Life* (Yale University Press, New Haven, 2001).

Sarton G., *Ancient science through the Golden Age of Greece* (Dover, 1993).

Sawyer P., *The Oxford Illustrated Story of the Vikings* (Oxford University Press, 1997).

Seward D., Eleanor of Aquitaine, the Mother Queen (Dorset, New York, 1978).

Swinchatt J. and Howell D.G., *The Winemaker's Dance* (University of California Press, Berkeley, 2004).

Taber G.M., *Judgment of Paris: California versus France and the Wine Tasting that Changed the World* (Simon and Schuster, New York, 2005).

Thorpe L. (translated), *Gregory of Tours: History of the Franks*, (Penguin, 1974).

Timberlake J.H., *Prohibition and the Progressive Movement* (Harvard University Press, Cambridge MA 1963).

Turner P. and Coulter C.R., *Dictionary of Ancient Deities* (Oxford University Press, 2000).

Vallee B.L., *Alcohol in the Western World* (Scientific American, June 1998).

Warburton C., *The Economic Results of Prohibition* (Columbia University Press, New York, 1932).

Weir A., *A Life: Eleanor of Aquitaine* (Ballantine, New York, 1999).

Zinsser H., *Rats, Lice, and History* (Black Dog and Leventhal, New York, 1996).

INDEX

Printed in the United States
65265LVS00003B/102

9 780875 864761